THE ~~HQ~~ Vera-Gray, F., **C**

How ~~1237~~ author. /

~~.V47~~ The right amount

~~2018~~ of panic

First published in Great Britain in 2018 by

Policy Press
University of Bristol
1-9 Old Park Hill
Bristol
BS2 8BB
UK
t: +44 (0)117 954 5940
pp-info@bristol.ac.uk
www.policypress.co.uk

North America office:
Policy Press
c/o The University of Chicago Press
1427 East 60th Street
Chicago, IL 60637, USA
t: +1 773 702 7700
f: +1 773 702 9756
sales@press.uchicago.edu
www.press.uchicago.edu

© Policy Press 2018

British Library Cataloguing in Publication Data
A catalogue record for this book is available from the British Library.

Library of Congress Cataloging-in-Publication Data
A catalog record for this book has been requested.

ISBN 978-1-4473-4229-8 paperback
ISBN 978-1-4473-4231-1 ePub
ISBN 978-1-4473-4232-8 Mobi
ISBN 978-1-4473-4230-4 ePdf

Cover design by Christopher Landry
Printed and bound in Great Britain by TJ International, Padstow
Policy Press uses environmentally responsible print partners

MIX
Paper from
responsible sources
FSC
www.fsc.org
FSC® C013604

For Lucy-bug.

May you always be as free as you are now.

Contents

Acknowledgements

Thank you to every woman who trusted me with your experiences, your thoughts, and feelings. I've been working with your words for so long now it feels like your stories are part of my own.

Thank you to my feminist mentors, Liz Kelly, Clare McGlynn, Nicole Westmarland, Maria Garner, Jo Wilson and Rosa Knight. You are my favourite thinkers. To Jan Jordan, Lauren Caulfield and Nicola Gavey, thank you for your wise words and insight. To the team at Policy Press, particularly my editor Victoria Pittman, thank you for seeing the potential in a short online article. Also to the cover artist, Christopher Landry, thank you for capturing the heart of women's work in a single image.

As always, my love and appreciation go to my friends and family, particularly my mum who made a home for me in the final weeks of writing, and of course to Mark. Hi.

Being born a woman is my awful tragedy. From the moment I was conceived I was doomed to sprout breasts and ovaries rather than penis and scrotum; to have my whole circle of action, thought and feeling rigidly circumscribed by my inescapable femininity. Yes, my consuming desire to mingle with road crews, sailors and soldiers, bar room regulars – to be a part of a scene, anonymous, listening, recording – all is spoiled by the fact that I am a girl, a female always in danger of assault and battery. My consuming interest in men and their lives is often misconstrued as a desire to seduce them, or as an invitation to intimacy. Yet, God, I want to talk to everybody as deeply as I can. I want to be able to sleep in an open field, to travel west, to walk freely at night.

Sylvia Plath[1]

ONE

Introduction

Do you remember the first time?

Claire, a White British woman in her mid-thirties, was seven years old the first time. She was going to a party at her primary school but had forgotten to tell her parents it was fancy dress until the very last minute. Determined to make her something to wear, they rushed around the house, found a bin bag, and worked it into an outfit.

> So bin bag liner went to school. It was dark on the way back and it must have looked to someone going past like I was wearing a mini leather skirt or something because they wound the window down and went 'Wahay!' I remember thinking, what's that? Like what *is* that? I don't understand what that is? This was a very small estate where I grew up so I probably wouldn't have been more than about 200 metres from school. It was dark, the middle of winter, but it only would have been six o'clock in the evening, seven o'clock at the latest. I think that we probably had freedom at that age more than typical eight or nine year olds would now where everyone's getting picked up and there's always an adult to escort kids around. That risk.
>
> Anyway, I vaguely remember everyone getting really angry about it and almost a kind of, 'That's because it's too short. That's why, it's because of what you were wearing.' So there was an anger at how dare

these people do this but combined with an, 'Oh that would be the reason why, it's because it looks like you're wearing a short skirt.' So they shouldn't have done it but come on you've got to think about this as well. It was almost an equal weighting.

Delilah, a Black African woman in her mid-twenties, was older when it first happened, sixteen and self-conscious. She had been told she was overweight as a child and it had really knocked her confidence. When she was in her teens she started to lose weight and had gone out of her way to find a gym class she really liked.

I remember being on the bus, leaving the gym just reading a book and sitting there and the guy in front of me turned around and started talking to me. And I just thought it can't be at me so I kept reading. Then he said, 'Are you ok? I'm talking to you.' So I said, 'Oh no I'm sorry, I don't know you.' And he said, 'I just thought we could get to know each other.' I'm like, 'No sorry, I don't really want to get to know strangers.' And then when I got off at my stop he got off as well. That's when I thought, ok it's really dark.

This guy just walked next to me on my way home and I had to actually take a really roundabout route – make sure I was always on a main road and that I wasn't actually heading home. Which really annoyed me because I just wanted to go home, I didn't want to have to lead someone up and down the road. I asked him to leave me alone but he just kept on, the whole way he was talking to me going, 'I don't know why you won't talk to strangers. Strangers are only friends you haven't made yet.' Basically insinuating that I was being very rude and should give him the time of day and I was just very actively walking and then eventually I said, 'Leave me alone or I'll scream.' At this point I was next to a hospital and it was really busy outside and so I think he thought she means it, and he went and scurried back home.

I completely stopped going to that exercise class actually because it was at that time of night. I just thought I'd rather go earlier, go straight after school. Which is a shame because it was such a good class, but I just thought I don't want to have to run into him again or anyone else who might want to follow me.

I remember the first time it happened to me, or the first time that I remember. I lived on the same street as my primary school, and my best friend would get dropped at my house so we could walk there together. On one of these walks, or maybe on the way home, we'd made a detour through the park on the corner. I'm guessing we'd stopped to get sweets of some sort as there was a shop on the edge of the park. We would have been nine or maybe eight, under ten for sure as after that she left for another school. And walking through the park one day a man, I picture him in a trench coat, flashed us. It's this strange kind of murky memory. I remember the light more than him. We were in this little dark patch but on the other side the trees cleared and it was bright startling light. I think we knew even then to just keep walking, to not tell anyone, to laugh it off. I'd forgotten completely actually until part way through the study this book is based on, when I called her and asked if it happened. It had, she said. She thought it had. She'd forgotten too. What's the point in remembering?

Small interruptions, ordinary intrusions. Shocking only because they happened too early, or because we see the consequence; the way they change our behaviour. At the time these play out as so trivial, so common, we learn to forget them. Nothing *really* happened. Like Claire, like Delilah, we make changes ourselves, to what we wear, to where we go. Learn to keep an eye on the possible. Hope it won't happen again.

And what about you? If you're a woman reading this, when is the first time that you remember attention from an unknown man in public? Being told to cheer up, being stared at, a whistle, a car horn, a comment, followed, touched? Singled out from all those that now you've learnt to block or manage. Maybe forgotten like mine, made less important as we learn that it's all just part of growing up. What about all the times that you're not sure – you think that man might be staring at you but you couldn't say for certain. Don't want to be thought of as narcissistic. Don't want to be called paranoid. But maybe, you think, I'll just cross the road, duck into the shop, catch the next bus. Can't be certain, don't know for sure, but I'll walk a bit faster, just in case.

Maybe like Lucy, a White British woman in her early twenties, you've pulled out your phone to avoid being stared at, called someone to avoid being spoken to, stopped when you get off the bus, not sure if he's following, but you wait back to see. The work of being a woman in public.

> I try not to look at people, like I look at them to see where they are and who they are but I don't look at them in the eye. I look straight ahead. And a lot of the time if I'm walking late at night I carry my keys between my hand, so I can stab. I think my mum's friend told us to do that. And try to stand quite big as though I'm tough and can handle myself. And don't really respond to people. If someone says something sometimes what I try to do is be quite polite but stop the interaction quickly, because I don't want to make them angry as well. So I've got to be polite but not too polite that they want to continue talking to me. And walk very fast, look like I know what I'm doing.
>
> Sometimes I pretend to talk on the phone. Me and my friends a lot of the time will ring each other the whole way home, so both of you talking while you're walking to different places. And every time we leave somewhere you have to text everyone to say you got home and if you don't one of the girls will get really worried. Then sometimes I'll just pretend to talk on the phone, if no one's awake or it's really late. Also I try not to sit next to a man. Because I've had people on public transport grabbing or touching you, but I'm never sure if they're actually doing it or, like a lot of the time the tube's really packed and I feel like, 'Is that guy touching me?', but I'm not really sure if he is. You don't know what's going on. Oh and

> I always make sure, it's really weird but if someone gets off at the same stop as me, I always think they're following me. So I try and stop or maybe that's when I pretend to phone someone, or I look in my bag so then they'll go in front.

Maybe like Becky, also White British and in her early twenties, you've told them to fuck off, changed buses when you didn't need to, crossed the street, avoided eye contact.

> It's one of those things where if I had to I would cross the street to avoid them, play with my phone. I do that with lots of men that I think might say something. I'll try to cross the street but again you don't want to make it obvious that you're crossing the street because of them, because that in itself can attract their attention if you did that. I never make eye contact, I just look straight ahead where I'm going. I have responded in the past with 'fuck off you pervert', which often works with men in vans but then they often yell back, then you'll get, 'You're a prude', 'You're frigid'. It happened to me recently where someone sat down next to me and he was staring at me, drunkenly staring at me, and I was trying not to make eye contact with him and he kept trying to talk to me and I was just ignoring him and in the end I just got off the bus because I didn't want to be in that situation. Which was an annoying thing to do because then I had to wait for another one which isn't ideal but I just didn't want to stay there.

Despite the commonality, or perhaps because of it, we rarely even think about the things we do. We don't talk about the habitual, sometimes unconscious, choices and changes we make daily to maintain a sense of safety in public space. The list so many of us have like Lucy and Becky. Different tactics, similar reasons. Or if we do talk about it we concentrate on the big decisions rather than on our ordinary resistance. We find it even harder to speak about possibility, this could all be in my head. He might just be walking the same way as me, I'm probably being stupid. It's nothing. How many times as women, as girls, have we thought this, dismissed this, always uncertain? How often have we second guessed others, second guessed ourselves, trying to read the behaviour of unknown men? Maybe a lot, maybe hardly ever. As Katie-Lou, a White British woman in her late twenties, explains, we're trapped either way.

> I suppose you just have to get on with it, don't you, because there's nothing really you can do. You have no way of knowing whether in that kind of situation, well I wouldn't know if anything actually was going to happen. So it's not like you can say – and this is the kind of thing that men won't appreciate – because I would say to my boyfriend, in fact I did say to my boyfriend, 'Some guy was walking with a piece of wood and slowing down', and he just thinks I'm imagining it, just like, 'Oh isn't she melodramatic'. But you know, you try it and see how you feel. I suppose it's conflicting messages isn't it? It's take care of yourself but then if you imagine that someone is maybe a danger you're being a silly woman. You have to do just the right amount of panicking don't you?

Claire and Delilah, Lucy and Becky, me, Katie-Lou – like most of the women I have spoken to – don't want to think of ourselves as constantly on guard. Scanning our environment, scared. We were, we are, powerful, intelligent, *empowered*, 21st century women right? We'd loudly proclaim a woman should be able to walk anywhere, wear anything, be anyone, without fear of violence. And we'd mean it. I mean we should, right? We should. But we don't. Not really.

When we think about it, how often are we thinking about *it*. That unspoken possibility. That known reality. We change ourselves, subtly, slightly. Small decisions to limit the chance. Sometimes, screw it, we choose to act differently. Take the shortcut. Stay and loiter. All of us just trying to find the right amount of panic.

This book wants to change that.

The Right Amount of Panic is about the safety work that women do daily in response to the reality and possibility of violence, harassment and interruption from unknown men in public spaces. It is about the fact that ultimately there is no *right* amount of panic, there's only ever too much or not enough, and with no way to know when we're getting it right, we're left unable to measure success. Trapped inside a catch-22, giving up our freedom and blamed regardless. But we're getting ahead of ourselves. Before we can change something, we need to understand it. Luckily, across the world, a number of women have been working to do just this.

The problem with no name

From large-scale studies to online and offline activism, we're starting to get a sense of the extent of the harassment that women and girls face in public. Often most common during women's adolescence, from the ubiquitous 'smile' or 'cheer up' to flashing, following and frottage (men rubbing their penis against women and girls in crowded spaces), such practices are frequently dismissed as harmless expressions of free speech, everyday annoyances, or too ambiguous to legislate against. And yet they comprise a huge amount of women's everyday experiences, as research is starting to show.

One of the most influential studies ever conducted on the issue was by a sociologist called Carol Brooks Gardner in the mid-1990s in the US.[1] Based on extensive research including in-depth interviews with nearly 500 women and men, Gardner found that all of the 293 women who participated reported experiencing some form of public harassment, and all but nine regarded it as 'troublesome'. Around the same time, another study conducted in London found that approximately 40% of women had been stared at, approached, followed or spoken to during the survey year.[2] Since these, a number of studies have attempted to record how common it is for women and girls to be interrupted by unknown men in public. Polling conducted across a number of countries found that at least 80% of women living in cities in Brazil, India, and Thailand have been subjected to harassment or violence in public.[3] Studies from Australia and Afghanistan both suggest that 90% of women have experienced physical or verbal harassment in public at least once in their lives, while studies from Canada and Egypt have found that 85% of women have experienced some form of what is most commonly called 'street harassment' in just the past year.[4] Alongside this, one of the largest multi-country surveys on violence against women and girls was completed in 2014 with 42,000 women across member states of the European Union. It found that just over half of the women surveyed had experienced sexual harassment at least once in their life, and that almost half had restricted their freedom of movement based on the fear of gender-based violence.[5]

But even these figures may not be truly representative.[6] Different studies measure different things, we forget so much that happens, and sometimes it's all so ambiguous – 'this could be in my head' – that we dismiss it anyway. This is where social media has stepped in to dramatically increase what we know about the forms and contexts of street harassment – how it happens – as well as more about what it feels like, providing validation and support for the experience. Two of the most well-known online forums for this are in the US.[7] In 2005, Emily May established what was to become the international *Hollaback!* movement, starting off as an online blog dedicated to collecting the stories of street harassment. *Hollaback!* now has chapters in over 30 countries, providing training, conducting research, and developing safety apps, including for online abuse. In 2008, Holly Kearl also started a blogging site, *Stop Street Harassment*, which has grown into a dedicated resource hub for research on street harassment, as well as launching in 2011 the international 'Anti-Street Harassment Week', and in 2016 a national street harassment hotline for support and information.

The use of online platforms to help understand street harassment extends beyond the United States. For example, in 2010 Rebecca Chiao launched *Harassmap* in Egypt as a way of changing the social attitudes that support the sexual harassment of women in public.[8] The project has now been adopted in over 25 countries. It works as an anonymous reporting and mapping system, with those experiencing street harassment, as well as anyone who witnesses it, able to send a text documenting what happened and where. The map and reports are used to create educational material which informs workshops and training taking place offline. *Harassmap* volunteers work with large and small businesses, transport companies, and schools and universities to help initiate and implement a zero-tolerance policy against sexual harassment in their spaces. This use of online reports to influence offline campaigning is also seen in England where, in 2012, Laura Bates started a small blogging site called *Everyday Sexism* to catalogue instances of sexism experienced on a day to day basis.[9] Initially hoping to document 100 women's stories, the project now has well over 100,000 accounts of the experiences of women and girls, and has been replicated in over 20 countries. The collective weight of these individual experiences has been used by Bates and women's anti-violence groups to successfully influence UK policy on areas such as transport and education.

The growing evidence from these online spaces is combining with research showing just how common harassment is in women's lives, to help validate experiences that were previously dismissed as unimportant or inevitable. This is fuelling a groundswell of women's resistance and activism, something that is spilling over into public spaces themselves. After realising just how few women she saw in Karachi's public spaces, Sadia Khatri started one of Pakistan's fastest growing feminist movements, *Girls at Dhabas*.[10] It began with Khatri posting a photo of her at a local Dhaba (roadside cafes popular in Pakistan), with the hashtag #girlsatdhabas. After posting photos like this for a few weeks, sometimes with commentary and sometimes as stand-alone images, she started to notice other girls and women were posting their own photos. Soon women from other countries were joining in, and researchers who had conducted a study on women in Mumbai's public spaces got in contact to say they had found something similar – that women were restricting their own access in public space; that they weren't just hanging out in public with no purpose or reason in the same way many men did.[11] The two groups joined forces and the *WhyLoiter?* movement spread, with women encouraged, once a week, to gather in public places and just … well … loiter.

The Katswe Sistahood, a movement of young women fighting for the full attainment of women's sexual and reproductive health rights in Zimbabwe, also brought attention to the issues through public action, leading a powerful demonstration in 2014 against the public heckling and harassment of women.[12] The protest began partly in response to the experience of a young woman who was stripped publicly at a kombi (minibus) rank in Harare, by men who claimed that they did it because her skirt was too short. Dubbed the 'mini-skirt march', the demonstration marked the beginning of the Katswe Sistahood's campaign to reclaim public spaces for women, making a clear statement against the policing of women's clothing choices and supporting their rights to bodily autonomy and freedom of movement. Back in the US, Brooklyn-based artist Tatyana Fazlalizadeh is creating street art to issue a direct challenge to perpetrators.[13] In the fall of 2012, Fazlalizadeh created the first poster, a sketch of herself with the caption 'Stop Telling Women to Smile', and pasted it across the city. She has since invited other women to be drawn, with their illustrated image used alongside messages speaking directing to men in public space such as 'harassing women does not prove your masculinity'. Many women have now taken part in cities including Paris and Mexico City, with the focus mainly on women of colour in response to how the conversation around street harassment has been dominated by white women.

These are just a few examples; however, taken together they demonstrate the ways that the experience of public sexual harassment is finally moving into the spotlight. No longer easily ignored as a trivial occurrence, it is starting to be recognised as a serious issue affecting the freedom of women and girls worldwide. So far, the movement has focused on raising awareness of the range and extent of men's practices, as well as highlighting the impact and calling for change. What remains largely unexamined is the range and extent of women's responses. Even taking the most conservative estimate that two in three women have experienced this kind of harassment in public, it is surprising that there has been so little interest in how women manage both the possibility and the reality of intrusive male strangers. With so much safety advice focused on telling women what to do to be safe (to be discussed in more detail during Chapter Three), there doesn't seem to have been much space to find out what we're actually already doing. This is the absence this book seeks to address.

Understanding safety work

The research this book draws on was conducted in the United Kingdom, involving 50 women from different age groups and backgrounds taking part in a three stage process of talking with me about their experiences of men in public, and then keeping a notebook over a period of two weeks to two months of different things they experienced in public spaces from unknown men.[14] We met up again at the end of this to go through what they had recorded, reflect on what they had said initially, and try to work out what we could say about it all.

The process asked a lot of the women who took part, from remembering and sharing previous experiences to actively challenging themselves to notice the amount of intrusion they experienced during the course of the study and the work they were doing because of it. This book is a tribute to their commitment, openness and generosity, as well as to the transformative possibilities of feminist research. Though a range of women took part, from different backgrounds, at different ages, and with a lot of different experiences, comparing their testimonies revealed some particular commonalities. Everyone had experienced unknown men in public space intruding, interrupting and harassing them at different times in their day and at different points across their lives, something that is to be expected for women who wanted to take part in this kind of study. Because of these experiences, those of friends, and what they'd read and heard, all of the women were also making habitual decisions about where to go or how to get there, what to wear or where to look, often without even thinking about it – not so much a choice as just 'what you do'. Again, this wasn't the biggest surprise, we all know that women do this, so much so that it's treated as common sense. The unexpected part was when women kept the notebooks, recording encounters and feelings, and reported back. For almost all of the women who used the notebook, they found significantly less *happening* than they initially thought, and yet were *doing* substantially more.

When I first met Alice, a White British woman in her mid-twenties, she spoke about how frequent men's intrusion was. She told me that she felt like she "can't leave the house without feeling constantly like I'm being bombarded by all these men". After completing her notebook however, she noticed a distinct difference, something that surprised us both:

> I think it was a feeling that didn't actually manifest as much as I thought it would. I feel scared and aware of myself and wary of men but whether, does that come to fruition? Not really to the same extent. Certainly not on a level I would describe as bombardment … but it feels like that because the threat level is technically, well the threat is always there.

For Abbey, a White American in her early twenties, it was the same.

> I think it was interesting that I don't get as many comments or as much staring as I thought I was getting. I think I maybe even said when we first talked that it would be weird if a day went by without this kind of interaction happening, but actually it doesn't happen every single day, or I might get some looks but nothing that would make me adapt my behaviour, that only happens every couple of days. So I definitely noticed that … It feels like it's happening every day because I'm always preparing myself for it to happen.

While the forms and frequencies of men's harassment of women may be different across the world, the work that women perform in order to limit it is constant. In short, a lot of women are significantly restricting their activities, limiting their freedom, in order to feel safe enough to be in public without being interrupted. It's here that we start to see the full consequences of those apparently trivial or minor annoyances. All those studies I mentioned earlier, 80% of women, 90% of women, all this research and online testimony speaks mostly to what has happened. What about the threat and the preparation, the way we adapt our behaviour? Where and how are we recording what we do to stop it happening at all?

As shown in the research that inspired the *WhyLoiter?* movement, one of the most common ways that women and girls cope is simply by removing themselves from public. A well-known study in Seattle found that 42% of women had avoided going out alone as a result of their fear of crime, in comparison to just 9% of men.[15] However, such avoidance strategies are not the only way that women change their behaviour. A poll conducted in 2016 showed that almost half of all women in the UK take a range of precautionary and diversionary measures while in public space itself – looking down, wearing headphones, dressing in dark colours – measures that often take place without much notice or fuss, absorbed as part of just what it is to be a woman in public.[16] This kind of work is not unique to the UK. In an autobiographical study, Iranian woman Fae Chubin, vividly describes the work she does in Tehran's public spaces:

> The sun is relentlessly shining over my head and directly into my eyes, making me scowl even more than I've planned to. I walk down this long, wide usually crowded street of North Tehran, avoiding glancing at the kaleidoscope of colorful dresses displayed behind each shop window. I, again, hopelessly search into my big messy brown bag to look for my sunglasses and to realize for the second time that it is not there. 'It's ok', I think to myself as I make a ninety degree turn into a bizarrely uncrowded street to take a detour, 'it would ruin the plan anyways.' You see, it is part of the plan; not to look around, walk kind of fast, show this intense sour look while you frown a little, making everyone know you are not the type of woman they can joke around with. This is the walk I have designed and developed through these years; the one that, so I think, would help keep me out of trouble in the streets.[17]

It is a similar plan to one used in the UK by Shelley, a British Asian woman in her early thirties.

> You've got to give off this vibe that you're just completely not interested in anyone or you're busy or on a mission going somewhere, doing something, you can't just be. You've got to have a book with you or look as if you're aggressive so people think,

'Oh she's probably not an easy target, I'll leave her alone'. Because as soon as I started doing that and realising I've just got to look like I'm a bit of a bitch, people stopped approaching me as much. It's hard work though.

It *is* hard work, though we rarely acknowledge it as such. Liz Kelly, one of the world's leading sociologists working on violence against women and girls, coined the term 'safety work' to describe these kinds of actions, the habitual strategies that women develop in response to their experiences in public. Strategies like Shelley's aggressive look or Fae's frown, like Lucy's keys between her fingers. Safety work refers to the range of modifications, adaptations, decisions that women take often habitually in order to maintain a sense of safety in public spaces. She describes it like this:

> We have become used to commentary on how women change their behavior in order to control what can seem like an unavoidable risk, but women's calculations and actions are more complex than mere self-limitation. I have termed the thinking processes, decision making and embodied watchfulness that women employ 'safety work'. It is work because it occupies time, requires energy and effort – all of which could be used for more rewarding activities.[18]

The idea that we have become used to how women change their behaviour is key to understanding why safety work is so often overlooked, both by the wider world and by ourselves as we do it. We perform safety work often without thinking, it becomes part of our habits, ordinary. And this creates a problem.

Take the example of Theodora, a White British woman in her mid-twenties, who told me that contrary to expectations about women and fear, something discussed more in the following chapter, she feels safe most of the time.

> I actually personally feel quite safe. The area where I live it's not, people say it's a bad area but I've never

felt unsafe walking around it. Maybe that's because that's where I grew up. But I've always felt quite safe to be honest.

This seems pretty straightforward, right? There's no right amount of panic here, there's no panicking at all. But the story becomes a little more complicated when Theodora begins to talk about what she does to maintain this sense of safety.

> I always walk really tall because I know I am tall. I think I'm the height of the average man so whenever I walk, I walk quite tall. And I do think a lot of the time people say, 'Just don't make eye contact', and I find a lot of the time the reverse is true. If someone is checking you out and they look like they could be quite dodgy, you've just got to give them not even a dirty look, not even an aggressive stare, just like, 'I know what you're thinking, I'm onto you, I'm just going to keep walking now, why don't you stay there'.
>
> Stop, check your phone, tie your shoe lace, anything like that. Always in a doorway though if you're tying your shoelace, don't get on the ground. Never, I would never. If I want someone to get past me I try to get my back to a wall. If you sort of stop and stand with your back to a wall and look at them, I never want to do that because I think it might cause a confrontation, but if you stand and sort of kneel down to tie your shoelace or something like that then it's a reason to stop if you see what I mean. As opposed to letting them know. Because I think if it gets to the point that someone's following you as opposed to giving you a funny look or whatever that's the point where it's stepped up in seriousness and you don't want to get too confrontational. But I would always put my back to a wall if I thought someone was following me.

What this shows is that the ability to create a feeling of safety through changing our own behaviour, means that sometimes crucial information is missed when we ask broad questions about crime and safety. We become unable to see the full impact of the sexual harassment of women in public because we've separated out safety from freedom and are only measuring the former. But in women's lives, the two work *together*. So much work that goes unnoticed, just to feel safe. When did we all start doing this, and why don't we ever mention it? Is it even making any difference? What would happen if we stopped? These are the core questions to be considered in the following chapters, and below is a bit more detail about what you'll find in each one.

Structure and contents

This book is divided into six chapters, beginning with this introduction. All chapters prioritise the voices of participants, with some quotes slightly amended to assist in readability. To maintain their anonymity, identifiable information has been removed and participant names may be pseudonyms. The first time a participant is quoted her race or ethnicity (self-described) as well as her age is given. At the back of the book is a more detailed participant list, including information on sexuality, which isn't mentioned in the text itself as it wasn't available for all participants. To help the flow of reading, notes have been used sparingly and appear at the end of the book. They include both references to academic and more general writing, as well as suggestions for further reading. For readers interested in a more conventionally academic text, including greater detail on the methodology and theoretical foundations of some of what is presented here, you can find this in a previously published book on the same study: *Men's Intrusion, Women's Embodiment: A Critical Analysis of Street Harassment.*[19]

Chapter Two, 'Women, fear and crime', explores the evidence on gendered differences in fear of crime, and different reasons for 'the crime paradox' given in feminist criminology. The paradox is that while women routinely report higher levels of fear about being a victim of crime in public space, crime studies show that men have a greater likelihood of actually being a victim. There are generally four explanations given for this; that it's to do with gender stereotypes; that it's about women's fear of rape; or that it's because crime statistics don't count all the types of crime women experience. This chapter addresses each in turn before suggesting that maybe what the paradox is telling us is that some of women's safety work is, in fact, successful.

Chapter Three, 'It's all part of growing up', takes us back to the beginning to try to understand how women's fear of crime develops and why women feel responsible for preventing our own victimisation. It draws on several large scale sexual violence awareness campaigns in the UK to explore how women are taught, by society and experience, that the cause and solution to sexual harassment is within them. These messages are then connected to what women learn in childhood and adolescence, that they are not the authority on their own experience, to explain why women express doubt about what is happening even while they are changing their behaviour because of it. It then looks at the ways in which young women are encouraged to 'take back control' by framing intrusion as a compliment, regardless of how it feels. The chapter ends in pulling these threads together to highlight how women are positioned as either paranoid or to blame for men's actions. Faced with these limited, and limiting, options, we learn to stay silent.

Chapter Four, 'The work of creating safety', gives real life accounts of women's different strategies to create a feeling of safety in public. It begins by giving more of a detailed explanation of women's safety work, highlighting its connection to other forms of invisible labour. Arguing that due to its complexity it is difficult to give an authoritative account of what safety work *is*, the chapter explores it by drawing heavily on the different practices and tactics that women spoke about. These are organised into three overlapping categories: behaviours that involve a change in movement, those that are about a change in clothing or appearance, and those that result in a change in being and the body. It ends in acknowledging how much of this work requires a reduction; women made to feel small and to take up less space in public.

Chapter Five, 'The right amount of panic', builds on what has been discussed in relation to the context and content of safety work, to explore in detail its consequences. It looks at how the individual changes women make over time, often made in response to the actions of men, can hide themselves in their habits. It uses women's accounts to identify the ways that many conduct an escalation calculation in public space to choose the safest course of action, as well as how this leads them into a catch-22 where women are blamed if they do not act to prevent sexual violence, but if they act and do prevent sexual violence they are paranoid for acting *because nothing happened*. Stuck like this, it finds that the only way forward is for women to routinely trade their freedom for safety, something that is hidden in a focus just on women's choices and not on the contexts within which they are made.

The final chapter, 'Ordinary resistance', concludes by suggesting that to get out of the double bind created by the right amount of panic we need to change the messaging in anti-violence campaigns, and actively create opportunities to acknowledge successful women's resistance. It argues that effective sexual violence prevention is not about changing individual actions but about shifting gender norms, and claims that creating opportunities for women to see the success of our safety work is one way to do this. It ends in suggesting that contrary to longstanding criticisms, feminist self-defence offers a way of unlearning what we've learnt. Helping us to create new norms of women as capable and rational agents, skilfully assessing and responding to the actions and motivations of unknown men.

TWO

Women, fear and crime

A paradox?

For many years, criminologists have studied how much people *fear* being a victim of crime compared to how much they actually *are* a victim of crime. This is done mainly through crime surveys which will ask questions such as, 'How safe do you feel walking in your neighbourhood at night?' and 'How likely do you feel it is that you will experience a particular type of crime (for example robbery or rape) in the next 12 months?' The answers to these questions give researchers an idea about how scared or concerned someone is about experiencing crime. These answers are analysed in relation to information reported to researchers and recorded by the criminal justice system about actual experiences of crime. The difference between these fears or expectations and the recorded rates of crime form the basis of what is called the fear of crime paradox.

Put simply, the paradox is that relatively consistently, across studies, across decades, and across contexts, women report significantly *higher* levels of fear of crime than men – often two or three times more – yet routinely crime statistics show that women actually have a *lower* rate of victimisation than men do.[1] This gender difference is by far the most consistent finding in all of the fear of crime literature. It also shows that those who report feeling the safest – young men – are actually the most at risk of being a victim of crime. Perhaps unsurprisingly, no one is ever really interested in why young men have such an irrational underestimation of their risk of crime. In contrast, a lot of work has gone into explaining what seems to be women's irrational fear. What the fear of crime paradox tells us is that gender matters as a predicator for the levels with which an individual will both fear and experience crime, but it does not tell us how. So what could be some of the reasons for this?

Typically, there are three main explanations given for the paradox, all of which may work together.[2] The first is that gender roles mean that women are more likely to admit their fears. Gender stereotypes typically attach vulnerability to women and fearlessness to men. As such, this explanation suggests that women are more likely to report their fear of crime, and that men may struggle to admit to a realistic estimate of how scared they are. The second is that the fear of rape or sexual assault is a type of fear that is particular to women. It is a fairly well-accepted statement now that across the world rape is significantly under-reported.[3] So the combination of this under-reporting of rape and the belief that this is the type of crime women fear most helps to explain why women report more fear but less crime. The third explanation looks to 'what counts' as crime, and thus what is counted. This says that there is only a difference between levels of fear of crime and levels of 'actual' crime if we ignore a number of experiences that women are more likely than men to have but that may not be labelled as criminal – experiences of sexual harassment in public for example.

I want to add a fourth possible explanation, based on the right amount of panic. This explanation works alongside rather than in competition with the others, and suggests that the safety work women perform *because* of their fear of crime may in fact be *reducing* their levels of victimisation. That it is not so much a paradox we are seeing here but a relationship of effect, where the fear is having an influence on women's behaviour and that this altered behaviour may be reducing the amount of crime they experience. However, women are rarely acknowledged as having any awareness about safety or danger. This is exemplified in the frequent 'common sense' safety advice we see given to women – advice that often focuses on constraining women's behaviour, something that research has shown may actually increase women's fear.[4] Combined with these external messages, women are taught to doubt how they make sense of an event, something that will be covered in greater detail during Chapter Three. As such, the idea that our actions may actually be successfully reducing our rate of experiencing crime is dismissed before it is even considered, not only by researchers but also by ourselves.

To give more space for the complexity in these explanations than these few sentences allow, this chapter will look at each in turn. Beginning with the role of gender.

Gender roles and the role of gender

At this point in time, gender is a difficult thing to define. While it can be broadly described as referring to the social relations, attributes, practices and opportunities associated with being female and male, recently the idea that there are only two genders has been the subject of great discussion. What has been revealed is this binary conception of gender – that there are only two – is pretty unique to the West. Many cultures around the world have always acknowledged a multiplicity of genders, some of which are about embodying both female and male attributes such as the 'two spirit' identities of First Nations people in Canada, while others introduce different ways of being altogether. While making gender a hard thing to define, what the current flux around the concept and its meaning does show is how the attributes, opportunities practices, and relationships it describes are not inevitable or fixed – what it means to be a woman in India today for example is not the same as what it meant to be a woman in 15th century France. Gender norms are easier to pin down as these do connect to the idea that there are two separate and distinct genders, the idea of gender most common in the West. Gender norms are the generally shared beliefs about what women or men do. They ascribe specific attributes, characteristics or roles to individuals because of their gender and are maintained by social approval or disapproval. They are also highly successful in reproducing themselves – we learn what is expected of us, are rewarded when we do it right and policed when we do not. Over time, the reproduction of these expectations starts to look natural, as just the way things are. It begins to seem natural that women are just more talkative because all of the women around us seem to talk more than men,[5] or that men are just naturally better leaders, because most of the leaders we see, of companies, of countries, of families, are men. Which means gender roles start to look natural to everyone else and even to ourselves – making them harder to challenge or change.

These gender norms, and the roles or characteristics they ascribe to women and men, are not universal. They are affected by other ways we are positioned in society, such as through our race. For example, in the UK currently while gender norms may stereotype many white women as sexually passive and many black women as sexual actors, this does not mean that black women are afforded more sexual freedom. Rather, black women's sexuality is routinely painted as wild or animalistic, something out of control or dangerous, and this construction is then used to locate them as *less than* on a hierarchy of worth that values women in relation to their sexual pureness. Another example is given by the eminent American sociologist Patricia Hill Collins in relation to how black and white women were viewed by slave owners in America, with white women seen as obedient dogs and black women as obstinate mules. She points out how both of these roles work to dehumanise women but in different ways.[6]

These raced and gendered stereotypes interlock with other factors such as class, age and/or disability. Again in a UK context, think about how working-class white girls are routinely stereotyped as sexually available rather than sexually passive. So that apparent universal norm of white women's sexual passivity mentioned above is revealed as applying to a particular type or class of white woman. White working-class women – along with working-class women of colour – are frequently stereotyped as sexually 'loose', reinforced by the preoccupation of talk shows and the tabloid press with working-class women who have multiple children with multiple men. This is then used to locate them in relation to the values of female sexual purity and respectability, setting what action is acceptable from them and, crucially, what action is permissible against them.

The term intersectionality was coined to describe this by Law Professor Kimberlé Crenshaw, particularly in relation to the experience of African-American women.[7] Crenshaw wanted to find a way to talk about how African-American women were unprotected by anti-discrimination legislation because it separated the causes of discrimination into parallel lines – either being about race or about gender – meaning that discrimination that was based on both at the same time, that existed at the *intersection* of both race and gender, was without remedy. She drew on a 1976 case where five black women were unsuccessful in suing General Motors on the grounds of race and gender discrimination to illustrate this. The US District Court found that because General Motors hired women (white women in administration) and African-Americans (men in production), there was no evidence to support the case for discrimination on gender or race grounds. Essentially the ruling was that black women could not prove gender discrimination because not all women were discriminated against, and they couldn't prove race discrimination because not all black people were discriminated against. The fact that there were no black women hired, and thus that there was evidence to support the case for discrimination on the grounds of gender and race *at the same time,* was hidden by separating out the forms of discrimination in this way. Crenshaw used the idea of an intersection to talk about how gender and race are lived simultaneously, an idea that has since been expanded to include other ways our structural locations position us in relation to each other, such as through our class or sexuality. In this way, although gendered expectations differ across women, all women are limited by them, as are all men.

Gender comes into the discussion of the fear of crime paradox around the idea of vulnerability. Gender stereotypes typically attach fearlessness to men: across different positions such as race and class, men are overwhelmingly expected to be strong, active and competitive. Research has shown, for example, that men are more likely than women to provide socially desirable rather than totally candid responses – that is, that they are more likely than women to lie about how fearful of crime they really are in order to live up to their role as fearless.[8] This finding seems to stick across studies with different men from different backgrounds. It may mean that a good part of the answer to the paradox is simply that men are afraid of saying how scared of crime they really are; however, this is not the only role that gender plays in our fear of crime.

Women and men, girls and boys, are also addressed differently in relation to our susceptibility to crime, resulting in women having an increased sense of the possibility of their victimisation. Evidence for this can be seen in how crime is represented in entertainment media, from books, to movies and television. Now first off I have to admit I am a big, big fan of the American TV show *Law & Order*. Something about the formula, the repetition, the resolution in a one-hour format just works for my television watching sensibilities. But crime shows such as *Law & Order* have been shown to exaggerate the numbers of white, female victims of crime as well as hiding the scale of white male offenders. This has a circularity to it: such shows influence what we think of as crime, meaning more shows depict crime in that way, which influences what we think of as crime. It's a system set up to reproduce itself.

The idea is that women's fears are heightened by stereotypical ideas and popular images of what crime is, who it happens to, who does it, and how best to prevent it. This has been called the prevailing crime ideology.[9] For example, a study that analysed the content of *Law & Order Special Victims Unit (SVU)* found that overwhelmingly rape was represented as something committed by a stranger, resulting in severe physical injuries or death.[10] Alongside this, although most victims were shown in a sympathetic role, female victims were more likely than men to appear to contribute to their victimisation in some way – by associating with the wrong crowd for example, talking to strangers, or using drugs and alcohol. Also the representations of victims and offenders were raced. African-American women were almost completely missing as rape victims, despite the fact that in Manhattan where the show is set, they are the group *most at risk* of sexual assaults. Offenders were also disproportionately shown to be white women when compared to crime statistics for Manhattan; white women comprise one third of the offenders on the show but just 5% in crime statistics. While the lack of offenders from minoritised groups could be understood as a challenge to the prevailing crime ideology, the authors of the study noted that several of the episodes analysed had 'hidden' the race of the white offender, often having a black male as the key suspect for the majority of the programme. This study helps to make sense of other research from America with diverse groups of women that has shown that the images women have of criminals are that they are poor, immigrant, minority men who are unknown to the victim.[11] The same groups of women from a range of socioeconomic and racialised backgrounds also saw victims as mainly white middle-class women, despite the fact that crime statistics for the area where the study took place showed that women of colour – who were the majority of participants – were more likely to be victimised than white women. Some of the reasons for this are to do with the stereotyping of white middle-class women as passive, submissive and unable to fight off an attacker. But partly it also has to do with representation: as the *Law & Order SVU* study showed, we rarely actually *see* women of colour as victims, even when we are these women ourselves.

This tells us that the differences in stereotypes or norms associated with women in different racial and socioeconomic groups are important to consider when we're talking about fear of crime and gender. Thinking about 'women's' fear of crime can work to hide differences *between* women; suggesting all women have the same level of fear or the same level of victimisation, irrespective of race or class. What an intersectional perspective shows us is that this isn't the case – that gender is always lived at the same time as other social positions. These then also have a role to play in our fears, our experiences and, importantly, how much society cares about preventing our victimisation or supporting us in its aftermath.[12]

Sometimes, however, there really is common ground. Consider for example how women across race and class boundaries are all taught in some way that we are not only vulnerable in relation to sexual crimes such as rape or sexual assault, but that we are somehow responsible for them. Viola, a White German woman in her early thirties, reflects on the role this might have in creating women's fear.

> I do wonder to what degree feminism and the focus on sexual violence in particular has heightened that sense of personal unsafety. So say for example, I'm thinking now about those really weird rules to keep women safe that you get everyone now and then from

weird women's agencies. I'm not even kidding, I've read a list of things not to do before that included you're not supposed to be in a lift on your own with a man. And it's like really? Do I have to worry about that now too? And I think sometimes these victim blaming things – Transport for London telling women not to take unlicensed mini-cabs – it's just like, 'Oh so now I can't take a lift with a man on my own anymore so I have to walk up flights of stairs' but if I do, and something happens it's obviously my fault because I was stupid enough to do that. To some extent that fear has been created.

As Viola indicates, girls and women are singled out for messages about 'stranger danger' and bombarded with often contradictory tips about 'getting home safely', something we will look at more closely in the following chapter (including the Transport for London campaign she mentions here). A range of personal safety alarms and apps exist to back up this advice, with many marketed directly to women – pepper spray that looks like perfume, lipsticks that are also three-million-volt stun guns, and even a range of sports bras that contain either a built-in knife sheath or a pocket to hold pepper spray … knife and mace sold separately.[13] If the statistics repeatedly show that not only are men more likely to be victims of crime, but that they routinely underestimate their level of risk, surely these safety products should be targeting men? Helping them understand how at risk they are? Helping them get home safely? The fact this is so rarely suggested reveals how these products about safety are actually about a particular *type* of crime that we don't think of as being a risk to men. This is where we reach the second explanation for the fear of crime paradox. An explanation that asks what kind of crime women are really thinking about when we say we're scared, and whether this is the same kind of crime that is being measured when we look to the reported levels of crime against men. An explanation that in essence is about naming women's fear of sexual assault.

The female fear

In the early 1980s a study showed strikingly high levels of fear of rape among women in a US city.[14] Suggesting this was attached to the fact that rape is perceived to be extremely serious and relatively likely and that it is closely associated with other serious crimes such as murder, the study found that most of the women who responded reported a period of routine or habitual fear at some point in their lives. This isn't universal – for example they found that there is considerable age variation in fear of rape, with fear decreasing with age. They were also unable to say anything meaningful about socioeconomic or racial characteristics due to the limits of the survey sample, in particular an under-representation of African-American participants – something that perhaps speaks to what was said in the previous section about who is seen to count when we talk about victimisation. The authors concluded that women's fear of rape, called 'the female fear' actually lies behind their fear of other types of offences. This was developed into what is called the 'shadow of sexual assault' thesis.[15] This idea is that rape operates as a primary offence, heightening women's fears of other types of crime. The suggestion here is that women report a greater fear of victimisation in general because of the over-casting shadow of the fear of sexual assault – a fear that is ever-present and as such 'shadows' or is attached to experiences of other crime. This means that when women experience a robbery they at the same time experience the possibility of sexual assault: this possibility is lived as an ever-present potential for women.[16]

This may sound extreme, but listen to how Hannah, a White British woman in her mid-twenties, talks about being robbed. Hannah and her friend were walking home one night and decided to take a shortcut down a poorly lit street. As they were together, they weren't really thinking about the possibility of sexual assault and so felt safe enough to take the back street and make it home quicker. Deep in conversation, two men came up behind them quietly, one grabbed Hannah's wrist to hold her back while the other pushed her friend forward to separate them. Then they dragged them both to the ground behind a wall so that anyone walking down the street would not be able to see them.

> And I remember thinking at the time, 'I've got no idea what's going to happen next', because you can't think at the time, you can't think, 'Are they after my money or are they after something else?' And I remember the one who'd got me, he was – well for a nicer way to put it, he was the nicer of the two men – he said, 'Don't worry we're not going to hurt you.' He didn't specifically say we're not going to rape you, but he did say, 'Don't worry we're not going to hurt you we just want your money'. Which I took to mean they're not going to rape us, not going to assault us. Which I still don't think was very reassuring. I don't remember thinking, 'Oh good'.

Being mugged as a woman was also an experience of the possibility of rape not only for Hannah, but for one of the men mugging her – who felt it so acutely he believed telling her he only intended to steal from her would be a form of reassurance. This suggests that women's fear of crime is different than what is being measured in looking at men's reports of crime – that the two are not measuring the same thing, as women's fear of crime is overshadowed by the fear of sexual assault. Lucy discusses exactly this in talking about her fears in public space.

> I think out of my friends a lot of the crime that some of the boys might have experienced is getting into a fight or getting beaten up which is a different thing to if you're walking along and someone attacks you or does something like that. It's not really the same type of crime. There's a different fear. And I know a lot of boys have been mugged which is sort of a bit different because you give them your things and then they go away. I mean they might be violent, but it's just that the fear of being raped, it's horrible.

Though different groups of boys and men may have different fears in public than Lucy's friends – a fear of fatal police violence for boys of colour, for example – evidence that Lucy is not alone in her fear can be found across different crime studies. It has been shown that when women and men are asked about non-violent crime their levels of fear are approximately the same; however, when the crime of rape is added, women's fear rises significantly.[17] Other studies have even found that rape is the crime women fear more than murder.[18] The research suggests this is because it is not just rape itself but the aftermath that women fear. From TV shows to news reports, rape is routinely depicted as *unsurvivable*. It is either shown as literally unsurvived (as in the inflated depiction in both entertainment and news stories of sexual violence resulting in death), or the aftermath is insurmountable. Like the earlier study on *Law and Order SVU*, we again see how the representation of sexual violence against women plays a part in women's fears. Though women are victims of all types of crime, they are primarily depicted in both entertainment and news media as victims of sexual assault. This can connect to gender norms that see what is important about women is our sexuality – and so the most important thing that can happen to us is something against our sexuality – as well as reflecting what we know about the prevalence of sexual violence: it is just so common in the lives of women and girls. However, the fear of rape is also connected to the ways in which women are positioned in relation to preventing rape.

Numerous studies across decades, across countries, have highlighted the frequency with which women and girls are routinely blamed in some way for rape.[19] Connected to what was discussed above around intersectionality and gender roles, women who act outside conventional gender norms of passivity, submission, and sexual purity – or who are put outside of these by virtue of factors such as their race or class – are afforded even more responsibility for violence perpetrated against them. The prevailing common sense view of the world as a just place – what the Venezuelan sociologist Esther Madriz terms the belief that 'nothing bad happens to good girls'[20] – means that fearing rape, and acting accordingly, is a way for women to show we are 'good girls': that we value our sexual purity and recognise the power of men. We are scared because we've been made responsible for preventing rape at the same time as being told it's inevitable. Sexual violence becomes a looming presence that must be evaded and yet is to be expected, and as such not being assaulted is often experienced by women as a *fortunate lack* rather than an unfortunate addition. It is lucky if it hasn't happened because it feels likely that it will. Both Theodora and Mariag, a White British woman in her mid-thirties, talk about this:

> I was very, very fortunate, I never had any horrific experiences. I know it's a really awful thing to say but I had the usual ones like being groped on the tube, and I do know in my mind it's awful that women feel like that's a normal experience. Like every girl I know has had it at some point, at least once. – Theodora

> You can have at that age a really precarious feeling of when is it going to happen to me? Not harassment but actual assault. When is it going to happen because I can't control it, I can't tell who is going to do it ... I mean that's the funny thing about rape isn't it, because it's reported as still this really rare heinous event but it's not rare. It's door to door. I've lost count of the number of women I know. It's systematic. – Mariag

Katie, a White British woman in her early twenties, expressed a similar feeling but in relation to rape not as a possibility but as a reality. While in Mongolia as a teenager Katie was raped by an unknown man in a park in the middle of the day. She talked about feeling something close to relief at having had "the worst thing" happen. Believing that no one would be unlucky enough to be raped twice by a stranger in public, surviving the rape gave her a feeling of freedom in public space, that, following Mariag, at least now it *had* happened, the wait was over and she felt back in control. We see from this not only that rape can feel like an ever-present possibility, but it also shows us how the sheer scale of sexual violence means that for many women and girls this feeling of possibility is based on past experience. Shelley explains this in relation to an attempted rape she survived as a teenager.

After catching a cab to the bottom of her road, Shelley was followed by a man who she believes must have been waiting around for a woman to walk past, and violently attacked. She managed to fight the man off and he ran away; however, the attack significantly affected her sense of safety in public.

> I definitely still have post-traumatic stress from it. I get flashbacks anytime I have to walk past there, which used to be every day. Whenever people are walking behind me I've got my back up now and even if people walk past me I'm watching them to make sure I'm in control. I think it just completely changed my whole sense of safety. I just learnt that women aren't safe on the streets. It's like if we're out and we're on our own, we're just fair game to men.

These experiences are not rare, and they do not sit outside of women's experiences of the potential or threat of crime. They are embedded in how we make sense of what comes after, and what came before. Viola, who also had experience of sexual assault, talks about the ways in which past experiences shape the meanings we make in the present.

> It works together doesn't it. You have an experience and then you make sense of that in light of the wider messages given out. So you see it in a certain light and that might maybe make you more fearful when something else happens or almost does, which then maybe makes you more likely to experience something in a certain way to make sense of it again. It's a bit like a vicious circle.

Viola raises an interesting point. Is it only experiences of rape, as both possibility and reality, that influence our fears? What about experiences of violence from an intimate partner? A father's regime of control growing up? What about all the things that count but aren't counted? How might these play a part in our fear our crime?

What counts as criminal?

Both of the explanations given so far – that gender roles and representatins influence our reported levels of fear, and that women's fear of crime is particularly linked to a fear of rape – don't really challenge the logic of the paradox itself. They both accept on some level that women's fear of crime is disproportionate to their experiences of crime. But what if, instead of trying to understand women's fear of crime as irrationally high, we ask why the reported rates of crimes against women are so low? If we start from the position of women's fear as legitimate, then we start to question whether in fact the paradox is telling us that something is missing from reports of crimes against women. Approaching it in this way suggests that it may not be a paradox at all. Instead it may be a result of what counts (and is counted) as criminal.

The violence that so many women experience inside the home, from childhood sexual abuse to violence and controlling behaviour from their husbands or boyfriends, must be considered for the role it plays in increasing women's fears of violence in public. In the United Kingdom alone, 85,000 women are raped and 400,000 are sexually assaulted *every year*.[21] One in four women will experience domestic violence in their lifetime and, on average, two women *each week* are killed each year by a current or former male partner.[22] Estimates published by the World Health Organisation show that around one in three women globally have experienced sexual violence in their lifetime – that's including both from a partner and from a non-partner – and over a third of all women murdered are killed by a male intimate partner.[23] Some of these figures are repeated so often that we lose the real sense of what they mean, but think about it.

Two women.
Every single week.
Killed by men they had loved.

Where's the outrage?

While men experience rape, sexual assault, domestic violence and domestic homicide – and have a lot of the obstacles discussed previously around gender roles and expectations to negotiate in order to have their victimisation recognised – the sheer prevalence of women's experience of men's physical, sexual and psychological violence puts us in different starting place in relation to fear. It's simply much more likely, and we know it. These forms of violence, though maybe perpetrated by family members, a friend or partner, affect women's fear of being a victim of crime, full stop. After all, the division between public and private violence really doesn't matter when you're just trying to stop it from happening again.

Similar to how women's experiences of rape as both a possibility and a reality (as a fortunate lack) influences their levels of fear, research has also shown that women who have experienced violence from male partners are significantly, understandably, more fearful of crime than women who have not.[24] So these forms of violence – domestic violence or sexual assault – most often committed indoors by men women know, increase our fear of crime outside the home by male strangers. And it's not only the fear they increase. Kirsten, a White European woman in her late twenties, talks about the impact of the physical and sexual abuse perpetrated against her by a boyfriend when she was 18, on her experience of being circled and heckled by a group of unknown men in London around the same age.

> It makes it more intense I think, it makes you feel more humiliated because you've got that from him, you've got that boyfriend, and then this happens on top of that. It just makes you feel even worse.

Jacqueline, a White British woman in her early fifties, talks about the impact in reverse, situating her early experiences of intrusion from unknown men as creating a conducive context for her ex-husband to physically and sexually abuse her.

> It wears you down in the end. That's what happened to me. It wears you down … You know none of that would have happened. I do think I would have

been subject to it at some point in my life but I don't think that my course in life would have been the same, that I would have ended up making some of the decisions that I've made. It wouldn't have been such a normal part of life.

Tracey, a White British woman in her mid-forties who has survived both domestic violence from a male ex-partner and a regime of stalking, threats of violence, and harassment from a male family member, talked about how these forms of violence from known men also prompted forms of safety work in public.

> Everything revolves around safety. Literally everything. Things are not simple, it's not as simple as just walking to the shops. Can't go to the park by myself as got to make sure there's going to be people around, got to make sure I don't walk past any dark alleys, got to be careful of time, if it's dark there's no chance in hell. Even the simplest trip to the shops I wouldn't walk, I'd take the car. So everything would be literally safety related.

These forms of violence generally committed indoors by men women know are not reflected in the crime rates that their fears are measured against. Even if they were, we know these types of offences are significantly under-reported. It makes sense then that women's fear is going to look too high in comparison – there's a whole range of crimes affecting that fear that just aren't being counted, crimes that don't fit the prevailing 'crime ideology' of criminals as always poor, immigrant, male strangers and victims as only ever passive, white, middle-class women.

Then there are the experiences that aren't really crimes at all. Think back to Delilah's encounter after her gym class, or Claire's bin bag. In either of these cases, would what the men did be counted as criminal? Not really. Of course most people would think catcalling a seven-year-old is inappropriate if not more concerning, but would they agree it should be unlawful? And it is equally difficult to imagine Delilah at sixteen being able to report being followed in such a purposely ambiguous way. How could she make the case against coincidence, that he wasn't just going the same way as her? Would any teenage girl really feel able to name what that man did as a crime? These are the forms that don't seem to count anywhere, but that cumulatively may be influencing our fear of crime.

While some of the practices thought of as street harassment are criminal (such as flashing or frottage), and some countries have managed to incorporate many of the more readily identifiable practices into criminal law, a lot of what street harassment is simply doesn't count as crime. Practices such as wolf whistles or cars honking, those prolonged one-sided conversations, being told to cheer up or smile, being forced to walk between two men who take up the space to watch you pass, these might not be criminal acts but they impact on women's feelings of being visible, conspicuous, vulnerable, trapped. Take the experience of Laura, a White British woman in her early twenties, on a flight from England to the US.

> Public transport is a great example where guys sit uncomfortably close to you on a bus and they'll just be really invading your personal space but you don't say anything because it might be busy and you're just trying to read your paper. The worst one actually was on a plane, this guy on a plane. Transatlantic flight so I was there for quite a while, completely stuck. I was on the window and he was on the middle seat and there was this armrest there and he was leaning all over it and trying to talk to me and I was trying to be polite and friendly but then because it went on for so long he was really just starting to get on my nerves. I just wanted to be left alone to watch my film or whatever, and he was constantly leaning over and being like, 'Where are you going?' and 'What are you doing?' and 'Is this a holiday?' and 'Have you got a boyfriend?' I didn't know what to do really. I guess you just feel uncomfortable and want to get off the plane but if you start to ask to change seats on a plane the cabin crew are going to be like why? What's wrong with your seat? You can't really.

Or of Lisa, a White British woman almost a decade older than Laura, with a similar experience though closer to home.

> I was finishing an essay at school and was getting the bus back and this very drunk man got on and he was getting off at my stop so I had to wait and get off at the next stop because I didn't want him to, well where my house was you could go the long way round or you could go down an alleyway which was behind some shops and I didn't want him to know that I was going to go down that dark and dingy alleyway. So I just got off at the next stop and went around. But the whole time he was talking about how he's had a really good night and then he was like, 'Oh do you have a boyfriend?' so I was like, 'Yep I have a boyfriend.' And then he kept pestering me about him: 'Where's your boyfriend?' 'Where's your boyfriend tonight?' 'You shouldn't be alone on St Patrick's Day.' He just kept going on and on and on.
>
> I really hate those situations because I really want to be like, 'Fuck off, I've just been writing an essay for the past five hours about a topic I hate and I just want to get it done. I don't want to talk to you anymore. Go and talk to someone else. Someone come and save me from this man.' But then you do think, 'Oh then I'm being rude, he's just a nice drunk man who wants to have a chat, and you just happen to be the person he wants to have a chat with.' You don't want to make a scene.

Or of Josina, a Black British woman in her late twenties. As a lesbian, the questions about her boyfriend are replaced with requests for sexual access to her and her girlfriend.

> Young boys like 14, 15 year olds, coming up to us saying, 'Are you lesbians? Kiss then.' And they're sort of young and working class mixed ethnicity groups and I just said, 'Look you're being offensive, you know you're being disrespectful, stop'. And usually

they have and said sorry and just gone away. One of them threw something but it didn't hit me so I wasn't really bothered. And then one really pissed me off, though my girlfriend had a different reaction to it. We were waiting at a bus stop and he walked past us and went, 'Oh my God, lesbians. Wow!' and got really close to us and was like, 'Oh are you two lesbians?' And I'm like, I really don't want to talk to you. I'm not saying anything to you. Why do you think this has anything to do with you? So I said to my girlfriend, 'Don't talk to him, turn away.' But he didn't go away. And then he was saying, 'Oh why are you being like that? You should be happy. Your girlfriend looks happy, why aren't you happy? You should kiss your girlfriend.'

Are any of these things criminal? Asking a stranger where they're going and where they've been. Asking about a partner or about your sexuality. Annoying? Rude? Intrusive? Sure. Illegal? Criminal? Probably not. But they should not just be dismissed as unimportant. For Josina this is about being acted *on* not interacted with.

It's definitely talking at you. It's not an interaction in that they don't want anything from you. I don't even think it matters to a lot of people how I respond. I don't think it matters to a lot of men. They feel like they want to say something and I can ignore it and that'll be the same or I can smile and that'll be the same.

It is this feeling, this understanding, that shows how these kinds of experiences are not the typical 'friendly' exchange between strangers that they are sometimes dismissed as (remember the man following Delilah? Or Lisa not wanting to make a scene?). This is not about engagement or connection – not a conversation but what Viola calls an *interruption*.

> You are more interrupted being a woman because
> people generally feel they can. There's this weird
> general sense whereby what women do isn't as
> important and can be interrupted. What women look
> like is much more important and everybody has a
> right to comment on it or have an opinion.

That these interruptions are experienced as ordinary makes it
particularly hard to capture in crime surveys, even where these
are counting experiences that don't usually count. I mean can
you really remember every single time some annoying guy you
didn't know has asked you where your boyfriend is, where you've
been or where you're going? Or has commented in your ear just
as he's walked past you, so you're not sure if he said anything at
all but feel kind of invaded all the same? Every time you've felt
as though some man might be following you, evaluating you,
intimidating you? Can you? I can't. I tried for a while to record
things as they happened, given I was asking other women to do
the same. I would just make a little note in my phone of what
happened and where, how I felt and why. I read them now and
they're like the words of a stranger, I can't remember any of it.
It's like Charlie, a White British woman in her mid-twenties,
explains, most of it is nothing special.

> I've spoken to some girls about it and they're like,
> 'Oh I don't really get it very much' and I'm like, 'Ok'.
> And then they're like, 'Oh but there was this time,
> and that time and something else'. And so there's
> something where you're just so used to it. It's just so
> part and parcel of being female. It's nothing special.
> It just happens all the time.

Not memorable, not extraordinary, but this doesn't mean there's
not an impact. Listen to how Sophie, a British Asian woman in
her late twenties, talked about the way these routine intrusions
affected what she wore, a strategy shared by so many women
it's covered in detail in Chapter Four.

I think I get stares and comments mostly. But I think there's something very powerful about eyes, they can really penetrate you. And when someone's looking at you in a way that you don't know what they're thinking you just know that they're looking at you in a way that makes you feel uncomfortable. It's hard to quantify it any more than that but it's unpleasant enough that I've been living in jeans and jumpers for six years. That's quite big, for me that's quite a big thing.

Or the way that Hannah talked about how they affected both her feeling of belonging in public space and her expectations of unknown men.

There's been days when I've not even thought about it, just carrying on doing what I'm doing, and something like this has happened and it's just completely knocked me, can't think straight, can't continue as I was, and it's just ruined my day because it's something that I feel has been targeted at me, even if it's just because of my gender regardless of whether it's targeted at me as a person, it just ruins my day. You can't think about anything else, because you think, 'Do I have to put up with this? They keep saying stuff to me in the street, am I not allowed to walk around?' And if I do see a man, I'm walking down the road and I see a man coming towards me, I am prepared for the fact he might say something to me. I've just come to expect it.

Shelley restricts the amount of times she's alone in public space, a small adjustment made by so many women and yet still so unnoticeable. The lack of our loitering.

I'll try to avoid situations where I am going to be on my own and guys can just chat me up. Like I used to sit inside this reception at lunchtime when I was waiting for my partner instead of standing on the street, because a few times I'd had it when people were just leering past me and making me feel really uncomfortable because you're on your own. But sometimes I don't want to sit in reception, I just want to stand outside.

Like Shelley, Jane, a Pakēha New Zealander in her late twenties, feels that the ways in which women are more interrupted than men, impact her ability to just *be* in public space.

What I sometimes feel like – and I know other women feel the same way – is that I can't just go outside and be there. I can't just walk down the street, I look at my boyfriend, the way he can walk to Waitrose and back. Round the corner to Tesco, into Tesco, buys some stuff, comes back. He's invisible in a good way, but then we're not, someone's got to make a comment, whether it's positive or negative. And the one thing that's always struck me is that I don't care if you find me good enough or not good enough. I don't want to hear it anymore.

The routine intrusion of women in public space acts as a continual reminder that men can do something *to* them without any reason or anybody intervening. Even though these are not criminal acts, the feeling underneath them – what they mean – may legitimately increase women's fear of crime.

What counts as success?

Reviewing responses to the paradox we can start to question whether it is really a paradox at all. Women report high levels of fear because we are trained to be fearful, and men under-report theirs because they are pressured to pretend they're fearless. Women report high levels of fear because we are taught to be fearful of a particular type of crime – rape – which we are told is bound to happen to us, will destroy us, and that we are ultimately responsible for preventing. We report low levels of crime because what counts as crime in so many of these surveys is not the forms of intrusion that we experience daily. And yet this is the exact type of crime that is influencing how fearful we feel. But what if, in addition to the explanations given above, there is something else happening here? What about that finding from the European Union given in Chapter One about how many women are changing their behaviour based on the fear of violence? This is not something to celebrate obviously – it's hardly a marker of liberation to have women's decisions about where they want to go or what they want to wear made in relation to men's practices. But given that's what a lot of women are doing anyway, maybe it is having an impact. This provides the entry-point to the last possibility to be explored, and the one that is so rarely considered. What no one ever asks of the fear of crime paradox: what is it that women are doing that means they are less likely to experience crime – or at least the types of crime counted in crime studies – than men? What if women are routinely, without fuss or even comment, successfully preventing crime? What if our safety work is in fact working?

Take a look at the list of strategies Louise, a White French woman in her late twenties, has for when she is alone in public.

> For example when I go home, I have a hat for when I get cold but I'll tuck my hair into my hat because I know long blonde hair tends to attract attention. If it's raining I'll get my umbrella and have it as a stick just in case I get threatened. Sometimes I take a key and I have the sharp part in between my fingers just in case someone attacks me. I'll have my phone in my pocket rather than in my handbag when I'm on the Metro and if I'm going out I'll put my important belongings in my pocket rather than my handbag because I know that people can come along and take your bag so you want to have things to defend yourself on you rather than in the bag. All these things. I guess though that covering up the hair is the one I do the most at the moment.

Or how Sophia, a White European woman in her mid-twenties, speaks about her external awareness, continually evaluating where people are in public space.

> I'm always very conscious that I don't want anyone behind me because it takes a little while to get the key in the door, that's another thing, I walk with my key in my hand and then like between my fingers. So I always take that out so I know it's a swift entrance through the door and if there's anyone behind me I'll always pop into the supermarket. You know I'll pop in and pick something up, milk or something small. Just so I can get out of the way and then come back out again.

Nisha, a Black Asian woman in her early thirties, talks about how her awareness of possibility dictates her movements in public.

> Like for example the top end of our street, there's a commercial building on one side and then where there's all the exits for all the stuff and there's all these alleyways, well not alleyways just kind of alcoves where the doors are, and I don't walk down there at night. I don't. I come in at the middle of the street not the top end. I won't walk down there because I don't know who's hiding in the corners. Because they could be, they could easily hide in those corners, and you wouldn't be able to see them and the bins there and the shadow goes right over the corner. And they could just jump out and get me and that's on my own bloody street.

Louise's work to ensure she has something to defend herself on her body is also limiting the potential for her important belongings to be stolen should her bag be taken on the Metro. Sophia is evaluating anyone who is "paying too much attention" to her, and is taking different actions to keep that person at a distance. Nisha's well-honed evaluations of her environment mean she's limiting her presence in areas that feel riskier.

If all of these women and so many more have their awareness focused externally, identifying points of safety at the same time as limiting their movements in spaces they identify as unsafe, then it may not be that men are more targeted to be victims of crime in public space at all. It may be that women are skilfully navigating public spaces, disrupting opportunities for victimisation by assessing the environment and individual men while attempting to predict their intentions and practices. This is what I mean by the right amount of panic. Women are routinely performing a multitude of different forms of safety work in public space that many men are not. Different women, at different times, acutely aware of our surroundings, tuned into the presence of unknown men. We are manoeuvring, adapting, negotiating our way, making decisions sometimes habitually, mostly unnoticed and almost always unspoken. What if all of this constant, embodied safety work is actually minimising the spaces men have to intrude? What if it's working and we are habitually intervening?

We know that it doesn't, it can't, work all the time and these times are all we can count. And then we blame ourselves for not getting it right – why did we do that? How didn't we know? But what about all the times you and I and the women we know have successfully prevented sexual violence and harassment? We may not be able to measure this, but we can measure what we do. The first step towards that is finding what's been hidden and that means going back to the very beginning: it's all part of growing up.

THREE

It's all part of growing up

Senseless and responsible

In 2015, a police force in southern England came under fire from feminists and anti-violence activists for a supposedly well-meaning 'summer safety' campaign. The campaign featured a poster of two white women in their early twenties, dressed up and taking a selfie, smiling. Underneath the caption read: 'Which of your mates is most vulnerable on a night out? ... The one you leave behind.' The moral of the story was clear: 'Many sexual assaults could be prevented. Stick together and don't let your friend leave with a stranger or go off on their own.'

The campaign was widely criticised as insensitive and victim-blaming, sparking a response from the police force responsible. Their intention, they said, was to highlight how everyone in the community should do what they can to prevent sexual assault, arguing that 'door supervisors, taxi drivers, bar staff and groups of friends or the wider public need to take responsibility to protect others from those who may cause them harm'.[1] And yet the campaign wasn't targeted at door supervisors, taxi drivers, bar staff or the wider public. It wasn't even really targeted at groups of friends. It was targeted at women. Specifically, at women having fun together. The underlying message is that our safety is more important than our freedom, and that though the police are there in the aftermath of sexual violence, we are responsible for its prevention.

The same poster, with the same well-meaning advice to men, is almost inconceivable. After all, men don't need to stay in groups to be safe, and if a male friend ends the night leaving

45

with a stranger that's often met with reward not reprimand. Yet women are continually targeted for apparently well-intentioned advice about how to keep ourselves safe. Don't leave by yourself. Don't leave with a stranger. Be careful at night. Be careful alone. Be careful in parks, on buses, in cabs. Watch your drinks. Watch your friends. Watch out.

Similar campaigns showing women in their early to mid-twenties on a night out – again frequently smiling, laughing, caught in that liberatory moment of women having fun with women – have been launched in the UK in the past five years by other forces including Essex, West Mercia and West Yorkshire police.[2] Despite the fact that across our lives women are most at risk from violence by the men we know, such common sense safety advice focuses on the threat posed by strangers – specifically, though unnamed, male strangers. The images of women in these safety campaigns are generally the same – mostly white, in their twenties, slim, single, attractive, similar to the women you'll remember from Chapter Two who are the most often represented as the victims of sexual violence in TV crime shows. And like those shows, these campaigns operate not just to set the women who we think of as most at risk, but also to signify the women worth protecting.

However, the police are not alone in this approach. As mentioned in the previous chapter by Viola, Transport for London (TFL) has also run a number of fairly infamous 'cabwise' campaigns to cut demand for unlicensed mini-cabs in the capital. After eventually ending a widely criticised poster run from 2009 which featured the face of a screaming woman pressed against the back seat window of a car, unable to get out, with the words 'Stop. No. Stop please, no. Please please stop... taking unlicensed mini-cabs',[3] they went on to launch an equally troubling initiative in 2014, encouraging 'young Londoners' on a night out to upload a photo of themselves on social media once they got home with the hashtag #homesafeselfie. As with the police campaigns, while the message was promoted as speaking to everyone, all of the campaign images featured young women and the 'safety' implied by getting home, was safety from sexual violence. Speaking about the campaign, TFL said that they wanted it to 'tap into the trend of friends and particularly young women texting each other to say they are home safe'.[4] Women's safety work here becomes naturalised as a 'trend' among young people. It is framed as just something kids these days do, denying its role as a rape prevention strategy as articulated by Lucy in Chapter One, and outlined by Carolyn, a White British woman in her mid-twenties, below.

> That for me was also ingrained from a very early age in that you always text when you get home. I mean even when I was at Uni, my mum was like, 'Are you going out tonight? Yes? Ok text me when you get home.' And that for me has just made me more aware, so I do tell all my friends if we're out on the town and we're heading home and going in different directions I'll always get them to text me when they get home. Not because I think anything will happen to them, but it's just in case something did.

Such a reframing of the meaning of young women's actions works to hide or even to deny the work they are already doing to 'stay safe'. In this way not only do such campaigns embed a fear in women in relation to their vulnerability to crime, a fear that as the last chapter showed can then be used as proof of their inherent irrationality, they also have the effect of infantilising women. The fact that our safety work does not – cannot – work *all the time* is taken as evidence that we're not doing it at all, and so we need to be told what to do, as Katie-Lou explains.

> Society doesn't believe that if you do take precautionary measures it will still happen to you. They think rape is because of what you've done because it suits their purpose to believe that it was somebody specific and their specific actions that led to that happening to them.

As these kinds of campaigns are focused on what is understood as reasonable advice (get home safely, look after your friends), the underlying message is that women lack reason. Criminologist Elizabeth Stanko points this out, as well as how such campaigns undermine the sheer amount of work women are already doing to secure their safety:

> This approach to advising women reinforces women's own sense that danger comes from random, unknown men, and it fails to acknowledge how much women's knowledge about danger already affects their daily behaviour. As one former police commissioner recently stated, it was necessary for the police to issue advice to women about commonsense precautions, such as to make sure they had gasoline in their cars prior to embarking on long journeys, because 'women aren't very mechanically minded' and thus, by inference, do not have much common sense.[5]

Through locating women as responsible for our safety, such campaigns also diminish the accountability not only of perpetrators, but of society and the state. This makes it harder to draw connections between, for example, stereotypes about what it is to be a man, what it is to be a woman, and how these gender norms set up what has been called a 'conducive context' for violence against women.[6] It also hides the impact of government policies such as, until recently in England, a lack of mandated education on sex and relationships. This makes it harder to situate experiences of men's violence against women as a cause and consequence of gender inequality, rendering it instead an individual problem with an individual solution. And yet it is within this social context, of gender inequality and restrictive gender norms, that the messages of these campaigns are received. They combine with media representations and women's own experiences to teach women we are constantly in danger and are responsible for stopping crimes against us. For both Viola and Claire, these lessons – of women and girls as weaker, vulnerable – begin in childhood.

> I do think you get these messages from very early on. So being a girl there's all sorts of things that are too dangerous for you, so climbing a tree or God knows what, just silly things. I remember my younger brother used to be able to stay out later at an earlier

age than I did, or watch crime shows on telly earlier than I did. And to a certain extent it's, you know, with younger siblings parents have relaxed a little bit, but I do think it's a gendered thing as well. – Viola

It just gets hammered into you from a really early age that this is how you prevent something from happening to you. You need to do the following things: you have to be careful about what time you're walking around, what time of night, always make sure someone knows where you're going and that kind of thing. I think there's always that and it's hammered in from such an early age, the stranger danger thing. – Claire

Ginger, a White Lithuanian woman in her early twenties, feels the same. Ginger started to see the pattern in the messages she'd received since she was a child when trying to explain to a male friend how she felt in public. After discussing several online blogs where women and girls share their stories of harassment, she started to make connections between how she felt now and what she'd learnt in childhood.

I was trying to explain to him how it feels for a woman to go outside in the street every day that you always – so automatically you don't even think about it – all the times you assess potential threats. And his comment on that was, 'Don't you think reading all this stuff online makes you feel a bit paranoid?' But no, no it doesn't because I've been thinking about this forever, I just never realised. Since I was four years old, living in the countryside. My grandfather would always remind me not to walk outside after dark. And it is countryside, there's literally 1,000 people, everyone knows each other, there's one street with asphalt on it, and there's one shop that's open for three hours a day. And I thought that that's just so weird. It seems like sometimes people don't really understand the implications of what they're saying to you, how far it will go. And then you have somebody like my friend who actually doesn't understand that's happening all the time, that I'm under threat all the time because I feel like I have to be.

The argument here is not that boys and young men aren't given the same warnings, particularly when they're younger. In fact, if you look at sexual violence prevention and awareness campaigns targeted to pre-teens, you'll find that many of these adopt a much more gender-neutral approach and – perhaps not unconnected to this – involve significantly less victim accountability than those targeted at adolescents and adults. But when we come to unpick how these messages are reinforced across women's lives, and how they combine with stereotypes about what and how women *should be*, we start to understand 'stranger danger' as being a gendered phenomenon.

A thought-provoking example of this comes from a study on children's fear of crime, conducted in England with young people aged 11–16 from working class communities.[7] Though the study did reveal that even among this group the fear of crime in public was distinctly gendered, with almost 30% more girls than boys reporting feelings of fear, when the results were broken down by age, the study showed something even more interesting. It was only from age 12 on that girls' fear became much higher than the boys', at age 11 *more* boys were fearful than girls (72% compared to 57%). As the research was interested in how codes of masculinity hindered men's and boys' ability to express fear, something looked at during the previous chapter, the study explored this finding in relation to how 'becoming a man' made it harder for boys to speak about vulnerability. However, the finding also raises the question as to how 'becoming a woman' makes girls feel more scared. Listen to how Ruth, a White British woman in her early forties, talks about her fear of rape in early adolescence.

I remember when I was growing up, so around that age, puberty like 13, 12 that sort of age, that I was afraid that I was being followed. Like I'd come home from school and we'd have to go up and get kindling for the fire, and sometimes I'd have to go up on my own and it was probably about a mile out of the village and I'd be a bit afraid, because it was countryside and there was no one around. And I'd think, 'Is there someone in the bushes?' A man, always, that was out of the question. And I'd imagine I could hear noises and that sort of thing and it would freak me out. But what I would do in those situations is tell myself that I was being ridiculous. That if there was someone there who was going to attack me or rape me, that someone wasn't going to hang around in some bushes in the middle of nowhere where no one ever walked past. And that's what I'd tell myself. That you're being ridiculous, that it wouldn't happen like that. But it was obviously something that was in my mind.

How did this fear get into the mind of a 12-year-old? Some of the answer here may be connected to what we've already discussed regarding representation. We know TV crime shows participate in inflating women's fears through not only their focus on female victims, but also in how those victims are held more responsible for what happened to them. Connected to this, as shown in the above campaigns, part of the process of girls becoming women is not only a continued focus on stranger danger well into women's adulthood, but an increased emphasis on the need to change our behaviour in order to be safe. In this way, women are positioned as more amenable and adaptable while the danger is promoted as consistent and inevitable. We become the only thing that can be changed, and so we *must* change if we want to be not only safe, but blameless.

This kind of representation of women, threat and safety can be seen in a 2011 resource created by CEOP, the Child Exploitation Online Protection command of the National Crime Agency, to ostensibly warn 'young people' of the dangers of sending sexual images. Called *Exposed,* the short film targets 14 to 18-year-olds and is promoted as dealing 'with the subjects of sexting and cyberbullying, issues that teenagers commonly face'.[8] The film tells the story of Dee, a teenage girl of black and minoritised ethnic heritage who has experienced what researchers recognise to be image-based sexual abuse.[9]

It begins with Dee in a hoodie and streaked mascara, crying alone in an empty café. She is soon doubled into a second more controlled and rational Dee, who appears as the voice of reason to talk through what has happened and how she can 'put it right'. After the distressed version of herself asks, 'What have I done wrong?' a flashback shows Dee beginning a relationship with a boy and, without any coercion, texting him five naked pictures of herself. Her boyfriend then shared these with a friend, who posted them on social media, leading to her being ostracised from schoolmates and friends, as well as being harassed online. The ways in which this story is depicted directs the audience to understand the problem as not lying in the non-consensual distribution of the images, but in Dee sending the pictures to begin with; pictures that, as she makes clear, she *wanted* to send.

Though the film is promoted as being for teenagers and includes a conclusion that speaks directly to both young women and men that 'you've got to always think before you send or share', *Exposed* isn't about the dangers that 'teenagers' face in the same way that the police campaign mentioned earlier isn't about 'groups of friends' protecting others. It is about young women. Specifically, young women having fun in a relationship, enjoying themselves taking sexual action. The underlying message is not just that our safety is more important than our freedom, or that we are responsible for sexual violence prevention, but that to remain blameless we need to be sexually passive – done to, not doing. This needs to be considered in relation to the discussion in Chapter Two on intersectionality. The different ways that we are positioned socially, through for example our race and class, interlock with how we are positioned as women. This means that regardless of their actions some women cannot be seen as sexually passive, they are made responsible immediately by virtue of characteristics they are not responsible for. At one point, when the crying and over-emotional Dee makes the particularly valid point that her boyfriend and his friend shouldn't have sent the images on, the rational and in control Dee gives her a strong reprimand to 'stop blaming everyone else'. Instead of positioning Dee as someone to whom a wrong has been done, the film quite literally locates her as both the sole cause of the problem, and the only one responsible for the solution.

Though an especially pertinent example, the campaign is not alone. Research with young people has shown the ways in which messages about sexual violence prevention can position young women as potential victims of men and boy's sexual actions, rather than as successful agents of their own.[10] Girls and women are understood as sexually desired but not as sexually desiring. When women are positioned as sexual actors, Dee's 'admission' that she wanted to send naked images of herself, they lose all claims to innocence. If nothing bad happens to good girls, then if anything happens to us we must be bad. This message becomes particularly damaging when we start to uncover just how early men's intrusion starts.

Girl, interrupted

At eight years old Cathy, a White British woman now in her early fifties, travelled by herself on a bus to see her older sister, about 50 miles away. Her dad had always encouraged her to be independent and brave, and she felt really proud she had done the trip by herself.

> So the following year I did the same trip but I did it with my brother. And we didn't want to sit on the same seats, we both wanted to sit on window seats, so what we did was sat at the back of the bus and pretty soon after we set off this man came on the bus and sat next to me. And he molested me on the bus on the back seat. And my feeling about it is that for me now I'm almost not even sure if it happened or what happened, the fear was so huge. Afterwards when we got there it wasn't like, 'Oh we got there', it was, 'My brother didn't help me and everyone on the bus didn't help me, they just ignored it'. I'm sure my brother knew what was going on but he would have been 13 and couldn't do anything because he was too afraid. But the other people on the bus, they didn't even turn around. At one point I began

to weep and nothing happened. And in the end the guy got up and went upstairs. And I don't know, I can't remember if someone did say, 'Go away, go upstairs' or something but I had this feeling of 'Why isn't anybody helping me?' I was really in distress. And so that's why I think sometimes it's like did anything happen? I just don't know.

Cathy's response to the lack of any action from those around her is uncertainty as to whether the encounter happened at all. It is a strikingly similar response to that of Luella, a White Latvian woman in her late teens, to what, like Dee's experience in the short film, could be called a form of image-based sexual abuse.

I've had men trying to take pictures of me. One of those things happened really early when I was about 15 or 16. I was just in a shop in my local high street, I was wearing a pair of shorts and I was just minding my own business, and this guy walked in, took a look, snapped his phone, took a picture on his phone and walked back out. It happened in the space of five seconds. And I was like, 'What?' I was just standing with my face to the wall looking at whatever was on there, and then I just turned my head, I saw him, he snapped a picture and then walked back out, he didn't run, he just walked back out really casual as if he'd just strolled in. I was so taken aback, I was just like, 'Did that actually happen?'

How are we to make sense of the ways in which Cathy and Luella, describing different kinds of intrusion, at different ages, and at different times, have this same sense of hesitation? Doubting their own experience despite their internal knowledge of what has happened. To understand this, we need to know more about the meanings given to these experiences in childhood.

Many women experience some form of interruption, harassment, intrusion or violence from unknown men in childhood and adolescence. These experiences can include verbal interruptions or intrusive questioning, following, touching, or, increasingly, experiences with unknown men online such as being sent unsolicited sexual messages. For a significant proportion of the women I've spoken with, these first experiences involve public masturbation or 'flashing', that is men's exposure of their penis. Cathrin, a White German woman in her late twenties, Josina and Mariag told me about experiences of being flashed as children.

> Back home where my mum lives, it's pretty much the last house before the forest area and it's on a hill and along the main street the town didn't think it was relevant to put a lot of street lights in there. So it's along a foresty area. We were quite young about eight or nine. But it was impactful so it was quite the story to remember. It was the middle of the day and some guy, very seriously in a trench coat, was following myself and a friend of mine from school halfway up that hill, in the forest, into a green space and then actually exposed himself. – Cathrin

> When I was much, much younger that's when I was flashed. It hasn't happened for years ... in a park with a friend aged 11, that's when I remember it happening for the first time. A guy was wanking in the bushes, me and my friend were picking off blackberries. But we didn't know what masturbation was. I mean maybe I knew but I didn't know that's what he was doing, I just thought he was taking a piss for a really long time. – Josina

> What would usually happen is it would be covered and he'd appear innocuous but then at one point you might look over because you're horsing around or chatting and then he'd move the coat or whatever was over it. And your first reaction, I often think of it as a visual reaction, it's like what's that? Or that wasn't there before, what is that? Oh! It's your dick. Also if you're that age you might not have seen any. I know for example a lot of kids see porn now, but we didn't

see any porn, maybe once as a teenager, never seen my dad's, probably never actually seen one, so the first couple of times you see one I think all these mental processes go like what is that? It's horrible and then something like what are you doing to it? Because usually they'd be touching it. – Mariag

As both Ruth and New Mum, a Turkish woman in her early thirties, describe below, for many girls flashing from male strangers occurs alongside harassing and sexually abusive behaviours from known male friends and family members.

When I was seven or eight, my mum had a new partner, and he would make little comments and things so therefore I felt quite uncomfortable around him. I can't remember what comments but certainly he would make, like, sexual innuendo or something that I found really uncomfortable and didn't really understand. I was like seven or eight years old, but still had this sense that I didn't like it. – Ruth

It happened in schools a lot. I'd forgotten that it happened in schools, but when I was 15 I remember this boy got out his penis and he was trying to make me touch it under the desk in class. And I didn't want to and I wouldn't do it and I went home and I cried every night for a week because I just was like really upset. But actually now I think about it even primary school boys used to get it out. They didn't know what to do with it though, but high school boys are terrible. Like we used to have one boy and he would do it when he would sit next to you in Maths in class, and then other boys like in the park or they'd whip it out at the cinema and try to get you to touch it ... the boys felt no shame, they were really open about what they were doing. It was more that it was your shame because they were doing it near you. – New Mum

This idea of shame connects to what Theodora talks about as a recognition, even at that early age, of her responsibility to prevent men's intrusive practices from escalating.

> I was on the tube again when I was quite young, and I was on the District line, you know where they have the seats facing each other? I was sitting by the window on one and then a guy came and sat diagonally opposite me on the corner of the chair and again, legs akimbo, whipped it out, had a go, and I could see what he was doing out the corner of my eye and I just thought, because there was no one else on the carriage, I just thought, I can't make eye contact with him because if I do he'll think I'm coming onto him. I can't make any contact with him whatsoever, I've just got to pretend that I can't see him. Just put the wall up.

Even at their first jobs, young women are faced with men's public masturbation, as Jeannine, a White Canadian in her mid-thirties, describes.

> I used to work in this big chain clothing store and we used to have, well it didn't happen very often but on a few occasions, cleaners would be like, 'Yeah we're not cleaning that change room because a man has masturbated all over whatever was in there'. Because we'd have female staff on some of the changing rooms, even if they were men's fitting rooms, and men would go in and masturbate and be asking for clothes and just so disgusting … We had to call the police on them sometimes, like in the store, if they wouldn't come out and were just in there for ages and it was very clear what they were doing, making noises, just awful. And it was really awful too for the young girls, because they were young like 16-year-olds we had working there, they weren't 25-year-olds who might say something or be like this is disgusting

and has nothing to do with me. They were young and were just mortified.

The message underlying these acts is that public space is men's space, that they are able to act within it in the same way they act in private. Anne, a White British woman in her mid-twenties, talks about the impact of all of this in terms of a sense of unbelonging.

> I've seen people actually touching themselves whilst staring, not full on masturbating but I've seen people touching themselves. That was on a bus again, but I was in England that time. And it's horrible, you feel like something's been taken from you. And it's like, no I don't want you thinking about me while you're doing that. Surely I should get to decide if you do that or not with me in mind but you can't have that control over that obviously. It takes all the control out of that space for you. It makes you feel like that space isn't yours anymore.

Though remarkably common, men's flashing and public masturbation is of course not the only form of intrusion women experience in childhood and adolescence. Luella, for example, spoke about being wolf-whistled at in her early teens, and at around the same age, Jan, a White British woman in her early sixties, remembers being blamed for her response to an unknown man groping her knee during a film.

> I was in school and I was in my school uniform and there was someone building their loft or something near so there was like builders there for 12 weeks and my friend and I had to walk past them every day on our way to school and on our way back, and every other day you'd get some kind of wolf whistling or something and you're in your school uniform. – Luella

I remember once in a cinema, I must have been 12 or 13 and I was sitting with a friend and a guy next to me started groping my knee. And I said to my friend, 'This guy's touching me'. And she said first of all, 'Don't make a fuss'. And I thought, 'I can't'. So we moved. But it was me making a fuss, not him being an asshole. – Jan

At 14, Josina was trapped in the road by men who wanted to get her phone number, something that, when we spoke, still felt like the scariest thing that had happened to her.

I think this actually might be the worst thing that's happened. Late at night I was with two friends and these two guys stopped their car because they wanted my number. We were on the street and we were trying to cross the road and they wouldn't let me get around the car, they kept reversing if I tried to go behind and pushing forward, so effectively trapping me as I tried to cross the road because they wanted my number. And I pretended I didn't have a phone but then took their number down just to get them to go away. And they must have been much older because they were driving and I was 14.

Add to these the accounts given previously, Delilah's experience of being followed from the gym, Claire's of being catcalled at seven years old, Cathy being sexually molested on a bus, and it starts to become harder to argue that these are isolated incidents. However, instead of this acknowledgement drawing attention to the fact that the problem – and solution – must lie beyond the individual girls, it is actually used to erase the problem completely.

We see this in looking to what is said to young women when they tell someone what happened. Jeannine, for example, like many other women I've spoken with, talked about turning to the women around her to help make sense of being wolf-whistled at on her paper route. What was this about, an adult making noises at her? What on earth could that mean? The message she received was common across women's accounts: that of men's intrusion as ordinary.

> I can very clearly remember the first time that a guy said something to me on the street, very clearly. I had a paper route and I was about 13 or 14 and this man was catcalling me from down the street. It's so vivid in my mind what happened. He was just shouting at me and whistling at me, saying 'sexy thing', and all of this and I was 13, delivering papers. It was so inappropriate. That was at the end of my paper route. I know exactly where it was, where I'm from, exactly where it was, near the pub and yeah him just saying, 'You sexy thing come here'. And I remember going home, talking to my mom, being very upset about it and she was like, 'This is life'. I mean my mom's very to the point, she was like this is life, you've got to learn to deal with it, don't react.

Jeannine was not alone. Jacqueline told me how she was flashed by an unknown man as a teenager. Like Jeannine she wasn't really sure what was happening or why, and told her mother about it when she got home to try to make sense of it all.

> When I was 15, I was walking up to my boyfriend's house and this man exposed himself to me, quite close as well, and I didn't really know what he was doing. And the police weren't called because, well I'm not sure why they weren't called. My mum said, 'It's all part of growing up'. – Jacqueline

Rather than blaming the mothers here for what feels like a dismissal, what both Jeannine and Jacqueline's experiences reveal is how sexual harassment becomes inextricably tied to the process of becoming a woman. When read stark on a page, responses such as this may seem abrupt but for many of the women who had a similar experience, they were understood as an act of care – a passing down of knowledge from one generation to the next, as Jeannine goes on to explain.

I think that's why I probably remember the first time so well, because it was like this horrible thing that happened to me and I have something to say about it, but from then on, slowly over time, it's become more and more normal, just part of life, your daily routine as my mum said to me. She knew.

What girls are being taught is what their mothers have been taught; the only way to cope is to reframe it, as complimentary or as nothing. Mariag talked about the confusion many young women experience in the attempt to reconcile how they feel with what they are told the experience means.

There's something about the experience of sexual harassment when you're an adolescent and you're both changing and forming your opinions about things, forming an opinion about what's acceptable behaviour between men and women or what's normal, what's good, what's bad, what's desirable, what isn't. It's a kind of a grooming behaviour I think because when you're impressionable it's giving you certain messages about what's funny or humorous and what's acceptable and what's flattering. Because that's the other thing, when you go to your mum or aunties or mates and they say to you, 'Oh it's flattering love, it's a good thing'. And you think, depends who you are, but you might be a bit conflicted then, because you think it didn't feel that way but apparently that's what it means.

Here we find the beginnings of that doubt. Maybe I've got it wrong, maybe it wasn't what I thought it was. Taught we are not the authority on what our experience means, sometimes the only way to resolve the uncertainty is to accept the meanings given by others; meanings that as seen above and with Cathrin below, frequently locate the problem as us.

It also made me start thinking about when I was growing up and when I started getting taller and becoming more womanly. I would notice these kinds of things happening and I sought out my mother to talk to about it and she said, 'Don't be so vain, don't think that they are looking at you and talking to you, you're just imagining this, don't talk about it'. So to some extent I thought maybe that is happening.

This acceptance comes for many during their teenage years, timing that is perhaps not disconnected from the shift in focus of sexual violence prevention campaigns during this time, nor from the increase in girl's fear of crime from 12. Understanding intrusion as complimentary at this age is an attempt to take control.

Teenagers taking control

Though their feelings often changed over time, many women discussed feeling complimented or positive about some forms of men's intrusion as a teenage girl. Support for this kind of understanding came not only from the adult women around them, but also from other girls and from their school environments, as Becky and Charlie explain.

I think probably when you're 11 or 12 you're not sure what to make of it and you probably think it's a compliment. I think I was lucky when I got older I had a friend who was the one who initiated saying, 'You filthy pervert' really loudly but I know a lot of the girls used to take it as a compliment, wave back and stuff like that. I really feel at school they didn't ever talk to us about this kind of thing or teach us how to be assertive, all we ever got was if you're wearing a short skirt what message are you sending? – Becky

I remember the first time it happened, I was about 11, and I was horrified. But after that I just got used to it. And I remember at the point getting used to the jeering and shouting, 'Alright love', that sort of thing. 'Alright gorgeous'. If anything, I was quite a shy kid and I was quite easily intimidated and I remember I was on a train once and I must have been about 13 and I was with my friends and we were travelling literally about ten minutes down the road, and a group of guys one of them pinched my bum when I was going up the stairs, and I remember I was really upset about it. I was really shocked and scared and none of my friends were. They liked it, they thought it was attention like, 'Oh look at those boys aren't they cute'. – Charlie

Understanding the experience as complimentary even where, as Mariag said earlier, this conflicts with how it feels allows young women to regain a sense of control. If it is a compliment then not only can you feel good when something happens, rather than shocked or scared as Charlie describes, but it is happening because of something about you, not simply because you are a woman living in a society that values you less than men. The choice is between experiencing what is happening as a positive evaluation related to your own decisions, or something that is being done to you and completely out of your control. The role of such limited options in how we make sense of what is happening is addressed by both June, a White British woman in her early twenties, and New Mum on speaking about the change in harassment over time.

I guess that in some respects it means at least in some way they find me attractive, but that's a really shallow kind of compliment. Depending on what happens, like if it's just a whistle or something then I might interpret that as a compliment because I mean, what else are you going to do? – June

I was also thinking about this because I went to have lunch with a friend the other day and she's in her mid-forties and I told her I was doing this and she said, 'Oh but when you get older nobody comes up to you and you're invisible and what's worse being invisible or that?' And I was like, 'I don't know do I have to make a choice?' But I have no choice, because it's not like I can control it anyway. – New Mum

When women are younger, this idea of the experience as complimentary is stated much more positively. In their late teens both Mia, a White British woman in her early thirties, and Marly, a White Swedish woman the same age, connected the experience to an acknowledgement of them as sexual and sexualised and, through this, a recognition of their womanhood.

When I was a teenager, early on, going to pubs and stuff, it was something really, not fun, I wouldn't say that, but it was this time of being 15 or 16 and being underage in pubs. I grew up in the North and it definitely went alongside really being a tart and you know how girls in the North East we really do go out with no jacket and no tights in the mid-winter, it's so true, and you would be wearing the skimpiest dress and probably looking awful but at the time thinking you looked sexy, and all these slightly loserish guys who were 36 in the pub, and you would think it was really cool. And I actually really liked that and I think personally it's really good for girls to go through that, to test your boundaries of being an object, testing that whole relational thing, and figuring it out and getting something between the leers and inappropriate comments and guys hitting on you. – Mia

I think I was 16 or 17, and I went with my Swedish friend who is equally as tall as me, we're both 180, and I was some wearing short skirts or something like that and we just got whistled at constantly and I think at that time it was the first time I'd found it happening to me and it was great, amazing, like oh my God. I came to the beach one day and got someone totally flirting with me and I was like wow, amazing, and I felt really positive about it then. An awakening of being reacted to as a sexual being.

Confirming something or bringing something out
in me that I'd never explored. – Marly

Though Mia and Marly are talking about different contexts,
Mia in her hometown and Marly on a language trip to England,
the commonality is clear. The experience of men commenting,
whistling, intruding is again connected to becoming a woman.
It is part of growing up. Here men are positioned as responding
to them, not at them; it feels like something that is within their
control, that they can play with or test. Such an understanding,
however, can be disrupted through experiencing escalation, as
Marly continues:

> But then I started school and I started going out
> more with friends and then I was in university for a
> year, so that was between 17, 18, up to 21, I think.
> And in that time I changed radically how I felt about
> that kind of attention because I had things like I had
> someone wanking on the underground and things
> like I was at a party and I left by myself and I had to
> walk through tunnels that I didn't know very well
> and this guy came up behind me and said, 'Oh my
> God you're so beautiful, is it ok if I walk behind you
> and touch myself?'

The growing awareness that she is not in control of what, where,
and how much men do, makes it difficult for Marly to hold onto
the belief that this is about her at all.

This is also seen where young women receive what they've
been told is a positive appraisal at times when they don't think
that they deserved it. For Abbey, this point came during an
experience in her teens.

> I remember in particular there was this path that I
> used to take to the library that was really quiet, we
> lived in a really residential area, and you had to walk
> over the highway at one point which I really hated
> because it was ugly and always desolate. And I was
> wearing like some ratty old jeans and a t-shirt with

like a rubber duck on it or something like that. It was just like the most ridiculous outfit, it was too big for me, it didn't fit me right, and I was walking on this bridge and a guy honked at me, and I just thought that was the weirdest thing because I was hot and I was sweaty and I was alone and I was wearing just nothing, like nothing exciting at all and I just couldn't understand why he thought I looked attractive at that point, because that's what I assumed it was, it was you look hot today, that sort of thing. I probably would have been about 15 so it'd be happening before that but that was when I, like that was the first point at which I just didn't get why I got it at that point. Because I assumed that I had to look good in order to get it basically, but I didn't feel like I tried at all and I still got it.

Like Abbey says here, when experience shows women that what we've taken to be complimentary is not really about what we look like, it's difficult to determine what is actually going on. Rosie, a White British woman in her mid-twenties, resolved this confusion through the discovery that instead of men responding *to* her, a result of something she was doing or the way she was looking, they were responding *at* her, regardless of her actions. It is a similar realisation to that Josina referenced in Chapter Two: the understanding that these practices are about being acted on not interacted with.

At 16 or 17 I used to like it as well. It actually was quite a confidence boost because I suppose when you're 16 and you're going to college you want to dress as nicely as possible because you're showing off your fashion because you're in the sixth form. And I don't know whether it was validation that, oh yeah, maybe I do look nice, even though it obviously was just men jeering. After the sixth form I stopped caring so much about dressing really fashionably or whatever and trying to like look nice all the time but the beeping of the vans still happened. So it was like,

ok now they don't think I'm that attractive, they are
just beeping at me.

The acknowledgement that women are not in control does
not help to alleviate the feeling of being responsible. Instead, it
makes it even more difficult to give an authoritative account of
what is happening. We are both to blame and paranoid. This is
vividly shown when encounters that are too frightening to fit the
complimentary narrative, are reframed by others as insignificant,
particularly when those others have the power to define what
is and isn't serious, such as the police.

Bec, a White Australian in her early thirties, has a telling
example of this. At 16, a taxi driver asked her to exchange sex
for her cab fare. She managed to force him to stop the car and
leave her on the side of the road, after which she flagged down
another cab and made her way home. She did not tell her parents
"because I did feel, oh maybe I had done something wrong",
but on talking to a neighbour, Bec reported what the man did
to the police.

> I remember I said to the policeman, 'Maybe you
> could help me, in the future if something like this
> happens to me Mr Police Officer what should I
> do?' And he went, 'I don't know, hit him over the
> head with your shoe?' And I said, 'I was wearing
> rubber shoes'. And he said, 'Oh well I don't know
> then'. Like, wow. I feel like a valued member of our
> community right now. How helpful. It was just like,
> 'Oh well you're a woman, I don't really give a crap'.

Instead of receiving validation that what the taxi driver had
done was serious and there were steps she could do to help
her in reporting should she need to in future (for example by
taking his licence or registration), Bec is told she needs to fight
him off by herself. The message here is not only dismissive, it
is that she failed to fight him off by herself this time, and thus
the problem is in her actions, not in his. Bec's experience with
the police is similar to Shelley's on reporting the attempted rape

she mentioned in Chapter Two, where a male stranger followed her after she got out of a cab on her street.

> I started walking quick and then crossed to the other side of the road to try to get on the other side, and he just came up behind me and got his arm around me and I just started punching him in the face and kicking and screaming and telling him to get the fuck off. I just went absolutely apeshit and he was trying to rape me because he tried to put his hand up my skirt. It was really violent and I ended up with massive bruising and my face was all swollen. He was hitting me back, he hit me back straight away. But he ran away in the end and I was still shouting at him as he ran away. It was literally right outside my house, like about ten metres from my front door so I went in and told my mum and she phoned the police. And it took them about two hours to turn up. So that's how seriously they took it. Not very.

Though there may be many reasons for the delay in police response, for Shelley the feeling that this was because her experience wasn't that serious was compounded by the lack of attention paid to her statement when they did arrive.

> When they got there they were rubbish. I gave them a description of the person and what happened and he would have had bite marks on his fingers because he put his fingers down my throat to try to stop me screaming so I just bit down really hard. So he would have had bite marks on his fingers and they didn't even put that down into the description in the papers. And there were more attacks over the next couple of weeks, just down the road, so it was probably the same person.

Bec and Shelley felt that the police acted as though what happened to them wasn't that serious, despite the fact that they had been told by others that it was serious enough to report.

This meant that not only did neither woman receive validation of the level of threat they had responded to, they also were both left unable to claim any success for the fact that their actions had in fact prevented further forms of sexual assault.

The culmination of all of this helps to answer the question this chapter began with. Having initially experienced intrusion as unsettling – outside of their control and to do with someone else, young women learn to reposition it as complimentary – within their control and about them. This teaches women to distrust our own sense-making of an experience; what you thought was harassment was actually a compliment. When future encounters demonstrate we are not as in control as we thought, we're left unable to be sure of our own experience. We are taught to doubt ourselves.

But the idea of intrusion as complimentary teaches something else as well. It encourages us to feel responsible for when something happens; after all, if this is a compliment and about us then we must be responsible for getting it. These two messages – women's inability to judge a situation correctly and our responsibility for what happens to us – are exactly those that are reproduced in so many campaigns apparently designed for our safety. The responsibility message in particular is further embedded through the pernicious myth of the world as a just and fair place, where as long as you are well-behaved nothing bad will happen.

Nothing bad happens to good girls

The lessons about women's accountability for encouraging and preventing men's intrusive behaviour sit within a social context marked by a particular idea of femininity. Gender stereotypes about how to be a blameless woman, position 'good girls' as those who don't make a fuss, who are polite and compliant, seen but not heard. Good girls make allowances, put others first, don't talk back, and this tells us how we need to be for nothing bad to happen.[11] Louise and Hannah explain:

> I think it's difficult for young girls who are unsure of themselves to say no to strangers. Because just

thinking of myself when I was that age, if someone came and asked me for a phone number or my name, I'd say no two or three times and because we've been brought up in a way to not be rude to people, even if the people are behaving in a way that's not socially acceptable, we find it difficult to tell them to get lost, that kind of thing is not socially done. So for example the number of times as a young girl that you end up giving your number but just changing the last digits, you realise that young girls don't know how to say go away. – Louise

I always feel bad about being impolite if they do have an innocent question or if they're just friendly and want to speak to people. I don't know whether it's just my personality or whether all women feel like that but I just felt like, he's harmless, he's just saying hello why would that be bad? Even though you know in your gut that that's what he's going to turn it into. He's either going to make suggestive comments or he's going to ask if you've got a boyfriend, as if he has some sort of right to ask that of you, it's a personal question. And all I've done really is left work, left the pub, going home, why do I have to be questioned by someone when I'm sat at a tram stop? Nobody else is being questioned. But I just feel this, just in case he's just wanting to speak to people, maybe he doesn't know how to speak to people and he's just trying to practise or something, on the off chance that it's an innocent intention, I don't want to be rude to people. – Hannah

Some of the women I spoke with felt they were much more likely to speak back when they were younger. In talking about this change over time, Sara, a White British woman in her mid-twenties, draws on a sense of being worn down – similar to Jacqueline's feelings in Chapter Two – while for Sophie, the change is more about wariness, grounded in a fear of escalation.

I think we've all been through something and it's one of those things you learn to bat away. When you're a kid you're more likely to face off with someone and get into trouble with them or start a fight or something, and as you get older you learn to, well, you learn to predict the kind of situations that you can be in. I used to be quicker to shout at someone or to respond to them in the way that they'd acted to me, so if someone accosted me I'd be quicker to push them away or have a row I think. I don't do that so much anymore, probably just because I've gotten older, so I'm more confrontational in different ways and less confrontational in different ways. I think with age maybe you have more self-confidence, you're more assertive. But you're also more willing to ignore things as well. You just get used to it. – Sara

When I was younger, when I was a lot younger, I was quite angry about things like that and I used to react and be like, 'Well, I've been where I've been what the fuck is it to you?' and I would say occasionally things like that and get quite angry. And most times they'd just respond defensively, like, 'Oh I'm sorry love, I was only asking', never anything more threatening than that, thankfully. I don't know why but my reaction has changed because I'm a lot less likely to angrily respond now. I would much more try to take myself out of that situation, because you just don't know who you're dealing with, you really don't. You hear stories all the time about people making the same bus journey that they make to work every day and getting stabbed or mugged or anything and I just think it's not worth it. – Sophie

Anna, Alice and Bec all changed the ways they responded to men in public based directly on their experiences of escalation. During her teens when Anna, a White British woman in her mid-twenties, received comments from men she spoke about being "really aggressive back"; however, after she was raped by a man she met on a night out in her early twenties, this changed.

> For me there's that fear aspect. There's a bit of a voice that's like this could get really nasty now. Because once you've seen that side of it, and that's what I hear you know, if I don't agree with them or I don't say what they want to hear, is that suddenly they're going to get really nasty. And so now if you ask what's changed from before then, from my early twenties to now, that's what's changed, I have a fear now that I didn't have before, because I didn't know how nasty they could get.

Alice was sexually assaulted by a male stranger in a takeaway shop who, after beginning by telling her she was beautiful and he was lonely, eventually came around the counter and grabbed her, biting her neck and squeezing her breasts, before she managed to escape. This experience, like Anna's, changed the meaning of men's comments in public.

> I think I probably felt much more regularly flattered by those comments before my assault than afterwards. Before my assault if someone said you look nice, that's a nice skirt, you've got a nice body, which I don't necessarily find negative because a compliment is a compliment and at the end of the day at the time I didn't find any threat in that but after that those men start to mean something different, those comments start to mean something different and those comments start to mean something that I can't control.

Bec learnt something similar through an experience of attempted rape by a male stranger. Bec was followed one night by a man that had initially said hello to her while she waited on a train platform. The man tracked her across several different lines and then off the train, with Bec only realising this when she suddenly saw him behind her as she turned into her street. He chased her, trapped her against a wall and attempted to rape her before she managed to get through her gate, locking him outside. Like Anna and Alice, the fear she felt during this encounter changed how she felt about other forms of men's intrusion.

> Before I think it was more like annoyed. Like, 'Oh can you just go away you're annoying me'. Or I would just ignore them. But now there's fear. And then I get angry that I'm so scared. Angry at them. At them making me feel like I can't feel the way I used to feel, just like free and confident and independent and safe.

It is not only violence perpetrated by unknown men that has this effect. Tracey told me how her experiences of multiple forms of violence from different known men, experiences such as stalking and domestic violence, also formed the basis for her response to intrusion from male strangers. Like Anna, Alice and Bec, the connection for Tracey is a lived one, drawn from the knowledge of what it is possible for some men to do.

> I get really defensive. I get really like, what are you looking at? Why are you looking at me like that? What do you want from me, what are your intentions? Then you start thinking, so just someone looking at you can make you really paranoid that you don't know what kind of person they are. You don't know what they're capable of doing to you. You don't smile back, you just look back in complete terror. – Tracey

The ways in which women and girls connect these different experiences has led to them being conceptualised as forming a continuum of sexual violence.[12] This is not about claiming a definitive hierarchy of seriousness from one end to the other, where for example the violence Tracey experienced from her ex-partner is 'worse than' being stared at on the streets. It is also not only about describing the spectrum of men's violence against women, the idea that there is a great range between what are still discrete individual incidents. Instead it is about the fact that the violence changes the meaning of the stares and the stares change the meaning of the violence. Seemingly 'one-off' incidents aren't really experienced that way at all. Like a continuum, the different experiences shade into each other; they are experienced *together* – it is cumulative and connected. This is why an individual incident can have a greater impact than may be expected if just thinking about the facts of the incident itself; why being stared at, honked at or catcalled can feel like a threat, as Ginger said earlier in this chapter. This connection means that the messages we learn in childhood stay consistent and become deeply entrenched. Over time this makes it difficult to say anything at all.

Learning to stay silent

'Break the silence' has been a familiar feminist call in relation to sexual violence since the 1970s. More recently women and girls have been taking to online spaces to do just this, not only through the activism mentioned in Chapter One, but also through tags such as 'my rape story' on YouTube, or #metoo on Twitter and Facebook. Though an important rallying cry for women to speak about experiences of violence without shame or stigmatisation, what can be minimised in this call to action is how difficult speaking is given the consistency in women's early lives of the message to do the exact opposite. Writing in the 1980s, Dale Spender identified the ways in which much of women's silence results from the limits of what she termed 'man-made language'.

> The silence of women has been a cumulative process. Conceptually and materially excluded from the production of knowledge, their meanings and explanations have been systematically blocked and their invisibility has been compounded.[13]

In the decree to break the silence, the solution again is situated at the level of the individual and this focus, like that of the prevention campaigns mentioned earlier, can act to deflect attention from the role of institutions and social norms in creating a context that encourages women's silence. In a similar way to how the question for women with abusive male partners is frequently some version of 'Why didn't she leave?' Not 'Why did he hurt her?' The question becomes 'Why didn't she speak?' Not 'How was she silenced?'

As has been seen, from the unsettling to the complimentary to the frightening to the ordinary, women learn that the experience of intrusion, harassment and violence from men is simply part of growing up a girl. The lesson, quite literally, is that these experiences are unremarkable. In childhood and adolescence when many young women do speak up, their accounts are dismissed or denied, and they are made responsible for what has been done to them. This positioning of women as either mistaken, lying or responsible extends from the most routine of interruptions to rape and sexual assault. Either we got it wrong and nothing happened or we got it wrong and it's our fault. Faced with contradictions between her experience and its meaning, as well as the necessity of preventing men's escalation, Cathrin explains how she learnt to stay silent. It is hard, she told me, to speak when the responses are some version of don't flatter yourself or that what has happened isn't really that serious.

> Combined with the don't flatter yourself, you provoke it – even at the point where you still wanted to share and have someone listen to your pain because it is ultimately pain, you were made uncomfortable in one way or another, whether it was just being stared at, *just* being stared at, or being touched or flashed or whatever it is – it makes you feel even worse when the person you're trying to confide in is telling you off in a way or ridiculing what you're saying or telling you to suck it up. That's not possible either. And then you just start to be silent, to not mention it. To forget and block out.

Clare, a White British woman in her mid-forties, talks about something similar. She describes how she connects the way she responded to an experience in her twenties, to the way she responded to the sexual abuse she lived through as a child – something she refers to below as 'the first time'. In her early twenties Clare was living near a tube station in London that had a long entrance before the barriers. It was around six o'clock and she was heading down that entrance at the start of a long trip home to visit her parents in the country. Walking towards the station barriers she was sexually assaulted.

> A guy came up from behind and attacked me. And stuck his hands underneath my skirt and tried to assault me or did assault me. I blanked out what I was wearing. Absolutely have tried to think about it since but have blanked it out, can't remember, apart from absolute frozen shock and fear and being too ashamed to tell anybody so I just went home. More than ever, more than anything else, what I felt was fear and shame. Shame that I shouldn't have gone out like that … but then also I think that some of the shame element links to sexual abuse, so I think that would be another reason, just to put it in perspective, that would have been another reason why I wouldn't have told my parents. Because I would have been blamed again. I was blamed the first time so it would have been further proof of me as that scarlet women.

New Mum also spoke about the connections between different forms; linking women's silence to our accountability, and suggesting this is why she didn't talk about being raped as a teenager by a boy she was dating.

> It's obviously happening to most women, but you don't talk about it. I think it's because you're told that everyone else will think you're a slut and no one will like you. Because I can remember this boy doing stuff to me and not knowing what to do, I can really remember not knowing what to do. And I was really innocent, I'd only ever really been with that boy before. But that wouldn't matter.

It is these connections, the ones that women make themselves, that mean campaigns encouraging women to break the silence about rape will never do what they intend unless they address the range of men's intrusive practices. The message cannot simply be report when the weight of experience tells us not to trust ourselves. The lessons women draw from our first experiences of harassment are those we take with us to make sense of what comes after. Jan outlines this in relation to what she learnt from male strangers telling her to cheer up as a teenager.

> So that was the beginning of an education in what it was really like out there I guess. That somebody else can control or has more entitlement over you than you have over them. And that you have to accept it and if you don't people will say you're making a fuss.

Other messages are translated between and across different forms. For example, the lesson in childhood that we are not the authority of our experience, the hesitation and doubt mentioned by Cathy and Luella towards the start of this chapter, makes it difficult to trust ourselves later in life as Nisha's account shows.

> I had a man wank off over me on the tube but I wasn't quite sure if he was actually doing it. He didn't touch me but I was on the way to work on a Saturday morning, like coming up to nine o'clock or something. I was minding my own business, reading my book or whatever I was doing, and I looked up and saw this man was doing something and I thought I'll just ignore him he's probably just some weirdo it's fine. Carried on reading and he looked, like he looked weird, you know when they look weird as well? And he was doing it and I was like fuck but he didn't have it out, it was just in and he was kind of rubbing. I felt like I couldn't move, I felt like I didn't know what to do. Do I get up? Do I move? Do I just sit here? Do I pretend nothing's happening? What do I do? There's hardly anyone else on the carriage. And I sat there for a bit and then we came into a

station and I jumped off. And I was really worried he was going to follow me. I was really frightened, like really shaken.

Despite the fact that she was shaken and frightened, Nisha still feels unable to claim with full certainty what the man was doing. Knowing that she is also responsible for preventing any escalation that would in fact confirm his actions, Nisha takes the only option available to her, she removes herself. When we learn in girlhood to dismiss our experiences of honking, whistles or catcalling, this doesn't just apply to these particular types of intrusion. The continuum of sexual violence teaches us to connect these forms to those deemed serious enough to be included in all criminal codes.

In this way, learning to minimise and dismiss the more routine forms of sexual violence teaches us to also minimise and dismiss sexual assault and rape. Across the continuum we are taught that it was either our fault or not happening at all, either we are to blame or paranoid. Hardly incentives to break the silence. So we learn instead to change ourselves, to limit ourselves, to take precautions. Repeated so often as to become naturalised, we forget the process behind it. All that's left is all we do: the work of creating safety.

FOUR

The work of creating safety

Invisible work

As seen in the previous chapter, at its core the lesson girls receive about sexual violence is that it's us, not them: either we've got it wrong or we've brought it on ourselves. The solution then – like the problem – is also us, and so we begin the process of making changes. This is the work of creating safety for women. Small alterations to what we do and how we are, that start young and, as Sophia says, just kind of continue.

> When I was about 11 or 12 I lived in America and at that age we had a high school that was quite nearby so I was allowed to walk home from school. It was probably about a 15-minute walk, but on the way there'd be construction crews I had to pass. And almost every single day without fail I'd get a wolf whistle, I'd get a comment, I'd get an 'oi' or something. They were trying to interact with me, and I was a 13-year-old girl, I was uncomfortable and I just tried to follow my route. But then it started changing and I started realising that, ok right if I pass by that group of men they call me so I have to cross the street now and I have to walk on the other side of the street. But then of course on the other side of the street a couple of blocks away there'd be another group. So it made me change my behaviour which I started to realise, for me it was just a 13-year-old trying to get away from it, but now looking back

on it I see there was something that was unpleasant enough for me to want to stay away from it. And that has kind of continued.

Though the extent to which we do it, and the range of strategies used, differ between women and across our own lives, safety work in any form is still rarely acknowledged, even by ourselves. For some women, part of the reason for this may lie in a resistance to the idea of women's vulnerability; after all, it's not only men who don't like to be thought of as fearful. Charlie touches on this in describing what is for her a lived contradiction: being scared and not scared at the same time.

> Even if I'm not, I try to make myself feel not scared and fine. Because I'm not actually scared, I am and I'm not. I'm convinced that it's not that likely that anything is going to happen to you walking down the street. And if it does, God that's awful, but at the end of the day, and that's where I think there's a difference between a fear of attack and a fear of people shouting at you, because I do walk down the street and, obviously I'm careful, but I don't walk down the street thinking, 'Ok I'm walking home tonight I might get raped'. I think some guys might shout something and make me feel uncomfortable or threatened. I am scared but I'm not.

We might not want to think about the limits we put on ourselves because we think to do so is to admit a weakness, or because we feel we mostly do what we want to do anyway. And if the changes we make are disguised and dismissed as just common sense, maybe there doesn't seem to be anything to talk about in the first place; like Theodora back in Chapter One, there's no panicking at all. But speaking about our safety work is not saying that all women are scared all the time, or even most of the time. Nor is it saying we should be. It is about providing a challenge to prevention advice that focuses on actions women could take, never acknowledging those we do. It is about repositioning women as capable and rational agents, skilfully and correctly assessing the actions and motivations of others. This is a form of work made so invisible it is concealed even from ourselves.

During the 1970s and 1980s the concept of 'invisible work' was developed as a way of bringing the range of women's work more fully into view.[1] One of the key studies looking at this was from 1978, conducted by a sociologist called Pamela Fishman. Fishman was interested in what could be learnt about gender through considering casual conversations between women and men. What she found was an asymmetrical division of labour in talk between heterosexual couples with women asking more questions, filling more silences, and needing to do more to be heard. Women were doing the work of the conversation, ensuring it flowed smoothly and felt natural, even if this meant they had to adopt a backseat in relation to their own views being listened to. Such labour was made invisible as it was a form of 'women's work'. As Fishman notes, being 'related to what constitutes being a woman, with what a woman *is*, the idea that it *is* work is obscured. The work is not seen as what women do, but as part of what they are.'[2]

The idea of extra work hidden as just part of what women are is particularly interesting when we take an intersectional perspective attuned to the differences between women. Judith Rollins' work in the 1980s speaks powerfully to this. Published in 1985, Rollins' study *Between Women* focuses on the forms of invisible work required by African-American women doing paid domestic labour for white women employers.[3] Where unearthing the invisibility of women's housework had previously been the study of sociological interest,[4] Rollins explored the complexities of the experience of African-American women hired as domestic help. She revealed the literal nature of their invisibility where sometimes they would be treated as if they were not actually seen by white women, who, for example, would turn down the heat or lock the door when they left as if no one else was in the house. She also highlighted the ways in which deference functioned as a form of work that was an invisible and yet necessary part of the role. Acts such as lowering one's eyes, slouching or speaking in poor English were required by the African-American women in order to validate the racial superiority of the white women. That such acts were understood by those undertaking them as a requirement, absorbed into part of the role, connects to the work of American sociologist Arlie Hochschild, on the management of emotion.[5] Hochschild developed the concepts of emotion work and emotional labour during a study of female flight attendants in the late 1970s. Emotion work, for Hochschild, is the work involved in dealing with or managing other people's emotions, and emotional labour refers to this kind of management done during work for a wage. As with Fishman's findings, Hochschild found this work fell largely to women and was rendered invisible. And just like Rollins' study, though invisible and unpaid this work was required, a silent embedded necessity stitched into the fabric of the role itself.

Keeping this connection to other forms of invisible work, 'safety work' and 'violence work' are terms coined by British sociologist Liz Kelly, to acknowledge the hidden yet necessary work women do in relation to sexual violence. Where violence work refers to the work women do in the aftermath of violence to rebuild their sense of self and belonging, safety work is the work women do as a precursor to stop the violence happening at all. She explains:

> Safety work can become an automatic reflex, especially when in public space alone as a woman: so automatic that we no longer notice the strategies that we use in our attempts to limit or avoid intrusions … a creative and varied set of strategies [including] that some women on some days choose to explicitly challenge the limitations.[6]

Safety work is hidden because it is related to what constitutes being a woman – not seen as something women *do* but as something that they *are*. And this causes problems not only because it renders what we do invisible even to ourselves, but also because it can mean we blame those who don't act in the ways we feel they should. Instead of an optional addition, safety work comes to be understood as a requirement and, as we saw in Chapter Two, these kinds of gendered expectations have a huge amount of influence over our actions and beliefs. When it is not performed, or not performed successfully (crucially the only times we can measure, as will be discussed in detail during the next chapter), women are perceived not only as having done something wrong but as *being* something wrong. Here we find the difference between guilt and shame, where guilt is about something we have done and shame is about something that we are. The ways in which safety work is hidden may be implicated in some of that hard-to-shift shame that spreads through the aftermath of sexual violence: if we weren't able to 'keep ourselves safe', the failure is felt not in our actions, it is in *ourselves*. Anne talks about this in describing the tension she feels between her right to freedom and her responsibility for being safe.

> If you think something bad is going to happen or you feel uncomfortable you are going to start to panic a bit and then you think, 'Oh is this my fault as well'. Or I knew I shouldn't have come down here at this time and then you start to blame yourself. Like I should have got a taxi, I should have waited for someone else to have come with me. But then it's like I shouldn't have to, I should be able to go somewhere if I want to, I have every right to do that without feeling paranoid or scared.

The contradiction Anne expresses here comes from the ways in which responsibility for preventing sexual violence is embedded in who women are, not only in what they do. This means that we can know on one hand that women should be able to act in any way that they want to, while on the other still feeling responsible if anything should happen. This highlights something that researchers have referred to as the difference between feeling safe from and feeling safe to.[7] The gendered expectation of women's safety work means that we learn that keeping ourselves safe *from* violence is more important than feeling safe *to* express and expand ourselves freely in the world.

This helps to offer an explanation for why some women hold female victims of rape accountable for what has been done to them that differs from that of false consciousness or internalised oppression.[8] Not only are women told fairly consistently that preventing rape and sexual assault is both within our control and relatively easy, we have more invested than men in believing our actions can prevent rape because we don't want it to happen to us, or happen to us again. Clare, who as mentioned in Chapter Three is a survivor of childhood sexual abuse herself, speaks honestly about this.

> I'm not proud of myself for it, but I will judge a woman who wears heels. I remember seeing a therapist once and hating her from the moment I saw her because I came in for an initial session and she was petite and wearing a figure hugging skirt, blouse, tiny kitten heels, and I had probably trainers on and I looked at her shoes and thought, 'I can't work with you, you're never going to understand anything from my perspective'. And I worked with her for about a year and a half and always hated her and never could work with her. Whereas previously I'd seen someone who had good solid German shoes on, and I was like, 'You're wearing sensible footwear, you're ok'. And at the same time I have a critical examination of those feelings, it's not just something that's unprocessed. I'm not sure if some of it was jealousy but some of it was definitely threat and some of it was not understanding why the hell you would physically restrict yourself. Why would you want to?

We see something similar in Cathrin's account below which reveals how the invisibility of our safety work can lead not only to blaming others but to blaming ourselves.

> I've been told off quite a lot recently too by friends and people that feel that they should be concerned because I walk home alone. I walk through a park alone in the dark. I do. I refuse to carry my key in my hand because it's a self-fulfilling prophecy. If you make yourself a victim and you project this feeling of, 'I'm in defence', you are approached by people differently. Even people that have no evil intention. I'm not saying that they're like all of a sudden, 'Oh my God I'm going to attack you because you have

your keys out' but it makes you more vulnerable and I don't ever want to be in that mind frame ever again.

The 'mind frame' that Cathrin is talking about here came after the encounter she spoke about in Chapter Three: being flashed in childhood by a man who followed her and a friend into the forest. Reflecting on this as an adult, she connects her experience of victimisation with the feeling of being vulnerable, but for her this vulnerability becomes the *cause* of intrusion and not its effect. The problem is reoriented from the man's actions to her feelings. The solution then – the way to be safe – is to never feel that way again, or at least to not appear like she does. Although her friends feel her behaviour puts her at risk, in reality it's all about safety. This shows just how complex this kind of thinking can be, the evaluations and strategising mostly hidden from view. This complexity means it is impossible to list definitively what safety work is. What the following sections will do instead is show the range of actions it can include, separated into the broad categories of moving, clothing and being.

Moving

One of the most literal ways in which women's freedom is affected by the need to conduct safety work is in limiting our freedom of movement, and this can start early, as Carolyn's experience shows.

I remember the first time it happened to me when I was walking home from school. I was wearing a skirt and I didn't normally wear a skirt and some guy just wound down his window and started shouting at me. And I think he poked his tongue out. And I think I got home and I just felt really demeaned and like I didn't want to wear my skirt again. I think I may have actually stopped, it certainly made me aware of what I was wearing out. And actually I walked home down the main road that day because I wanted to get something from the petrol station, but I didn't walk home that way again. I walked home through the park instead, not on the road because I don't want to get that. It made me change my walk home from school, that's how much it affected me.

Studies on the different strategies women use in public space have broadly separated these into avoidance behaviours, those used to isolate or remove oneself from danger, and self-protective behaviours, those designed to minimise risk when facing danger.[9] Both types of actions can be seen in the changes women make to where and how they move in public. Josina describes the feeling behind these changes, a sense that public space is not for her.

> Sometimes I can feel like the streets really aren't my own to walk in you know, like there's these men on there and they own it and I'm only welcome there if I accept that I'm going to be spoken to and they have the right to do that and to make comments.

Her comments here are reminiscent of Anne's description in Chapter Three in relation to men touching themselves on buses, something she said "makes you feel like that space isn't yours anymore". This feeling of discomfort, of unbelonging, supports the belief that the problem, and solution, is in women and their behaviour, rather than in the actions of men. We're the ones that have to change where we are and how we act, and we do it daily.

Like Nisha who in the last chapter spoke about getting off the train because she thought a man was masturbating, Jen, a White British woman in her late twenties, has changed carriages because of being stared at. For both women, the ambiguity of the intrusion makes it difficult to confront directly. As such, in order to prevent escalation, the only option, as Jen describes, is to remove oneself entirely.

> I've moved carriage before, once we got into a station, I got up and changed carriage because of being stared at. What can you do? I don't necessarily want to move seats on the same carriage because they know they've annoyed you then. But you know, I'm going home, I don't need this, I know what you're

doing. It really does annoy me because what can you say?

Ginger spoke about actually changing trains if she felt uncomfortable, along with several different but connected strategies about movement and placement on public transport.

> I usually try to sit next to women, at least nearby women unless it's the middle of the day and I feel confident not to, but say late at night and the carriage is empty and there's somebody sitting on one end of it, I'll make sure I sit at the other end; otherwise, they might think there's a reason to talk to me. A lot of times it's unnecessary because they're probably just as tired as I am. But just to be on the safe side, I'll make sure that I'm not on the same end. Other times I've waited for the person to get on the train. And then at the last minute I haven't gotten on the train myself because I thought that they were paying too much attention to me and it's safer if I just skip this train. I have actually changed trains in the middle, when I'm on the train and I know somebody's there who I would rather not be in the same carriage with. I get off in the station and I change for the next one that's coming. Even if it makes me late for something.

As Ginger shows in her decision to usually try to sit next to women, it is not only in response to particular encounters with particular men that women change their behaviour. Instead for many women and girls such changes become common sense, a habitual way of being in public. As will be discussed in more detail in the next chapter, for many women one of these habits is an attentiveness to their environment, and to the unknown men within it. Both Gail, a White British woman in her early thirties, and Alice talk about not taking certain routes home or to the shops, or taking them but with this feeling of constant external awareness.

To get from my flat to the centre of town you could either go the long way along the road or could take the short cut which was pitch black. And I know nothing's going to happen but every time I took that shortcut I'd be worried, that this is where people get murdered, this is where bodies get found. But you know I don't like to think that that's dumb, it'd be dumb not to. If this was a guy he'd be like, 'Why are we going all this way when you could take a shortcut?' But then you think if something did happen it'd be your own fault for taking the shortcut. – Gail

If I walk down a side street I'll be pretty fucking terrified so I don't really do that and I'll only do that if it's a pretty intelligent short cut. For example, Sainsbury's is two minutes from my house but I have to go down a back side street. Now I could walk two blocks to the main entrance but it's just so much quicker to go through the car park. However, if I take the car park route, even though I only have to walk what – 100 metres in the dark? – my senses are on overload as I walk past a car or if a man goes up there. I'll walk behind men but I won't let them walk behind me so if I feel like I'm going to be followed I'll move or I'll stop. I tend to stop with my phone and wait for them to pass. – Alice

This awareness is also seen in the accounts of both Lucy and Meg, a White British woman in her late teens, both of whom talked about feeling the need to restrict their circle of action for fear of the actions of men. For Lucy this came out in how she felt she could not enjoy beautiful, solitary moments in public space at night, while for Meg it meant that sometimes she felt she couldn't go out at all.

It's just really stressful to be scared all the time. One of my friends the other day said I love walking home through the city at night. I had to walk back from work because a friend couldn't give me a lift, at 1 o'clock in the morning. And he was like, 'Oh that's fine. It's nice to look at the river.' And it might be nice to look at the river if I wasn't petrified the whole time. I'm not going to stop and look at the river because I need to get back quickly so I don't get raped. – Lucy

I think some things like the freedom thing starts coming into play when you say like, 'Oh I don't really want to go on that night out with you because it will be really annoying getting home and I can't stay at yours, I don't really want to take three night buses through places I don't know and I don't want to pay £40 for a taxi.' So you just won't go, you'll go to your usual place which is on the bus route. Like a lot of my friends came up to London a year after me and they were going to all these new places and I'd just pass up because I thought I have no idea how to get home. – Meg

Researchers have termed this kind of interaction with the environment 'a geography of fear and limitation',[10] where in order to lessen the former, women routinely raise the latter. For example, Emma, a White Australian in her early thirties, spoke about enjoying running outdoors and yet the experience of being followed by men meant she had learnt to limit how far she went, making sure she was never far from home.

Once someone starts following you that scares you because I can't think of a good reason why someone would do that. There's no good reason. And it's just frustrating because it means I have to change to doing things only when I feel safe. So not jogging at night and wearing extra clothes when I'm jogging. I'm training for a 10k so normally I go quite a distance but I end up doing loops around home because I don't want to end up too far away, that sort of thing.

Jane had a similar experience. She spoke about the pleasure of running through central London, looking at the architecture and history, and feeling proud she'd made it to the other side of the world. Her experiences, however, including men calling out to her, following her, blocking her way, and trying to touch her, meant that over time this pleasure was lost and she ended up joining a gym so she could run indoors.

> I figured it out, my route. I planned through experience very carefully, like from coming back to going out I'd change it, there was this one road that coming back was always busy with deliveries because it was early morning, so I'd always go through the square. I used to go past a club but then I learnt don't do that, that's bad, but if you go past the gallery and another building it's ok. But then I had to change that because construction got up that street so that got bad. I had every street on my run planned out to avoid it as much as possible. I knew which roads. Now I just get on a treadmill and watch television. No more following. No more grabbing.

These limitations become naturalised – like Charlie said earlier, "*obviously* I'm careful" – leaving us feeling safer but unaware of the costs. It is only in considering safety and freedom together that the true extent of our work is uncovered, something that is revealed when clothing is discussed in terms of safety.

Clothing

Just as Cathy in the previous chapter wanted to share her experiences as a way of making sense of what happened to her on the bus as a child, Sophie wanted to talk about her realisation that she had been basically "hiding" herself to avoid attention from unknown men. She told me that since moving to London her experiences of public sexual harassment had resulted in her changing what she wore – even up to the point of almost getting to the tube station and turning back because she didn't feel safe enough in her clothes.

The amount of times I've gone out, say I've been meeting friends, and I'll get ready, I'll have this outfit in mind that I want to wear that I've bought specifically for an occasion, like a dress or something and I'll be like, 'Right I'm going to wear that', and it'll get to like ten minutes before and I'll bottle it, and I'll go back up to my room and I'll get changed. And I've even gone as far as the tube before, a couple of times, and had to turn back and go home because I just didn't feel comfortable.

Though she wasn't aware of it at the time, Sophie's strategy was not unique. For almost all of the women I've spoken with, some of the most taken for granted forms of safety work are to do with their appearance, particularly with what they wear. Both Anne and Jen discuss the changes they make to their clothing in an attempt to avoid men's intrusion, even with an understanding of the problematic message such changes support.

It's like you know if you wear a certain type of clothing you're more likely to get shouted at, and you shouldn't have to moderate yourself in that way but I do consider what I wear more. Maybe not on an everyday basis but if I know I'm going to a certain area where it's happened to me before or I know it's a bit dodgy, I'm more likely to wear jeans than a skirt. – Anne

It's stupid because it happens so many times and so many different occasions wearing from a short skirt to a long skirt and a winter coat or whatever, so I know that it makes no difference what you're wearing, but still some part of me has bought into this idea that you are somehow responsible for it and you can stop it by not wearing so and so. So I tend to change what I wear. I like clothes but I have certain skirts of a certain length that I only wear when I'm going out with my husband for example. Which is ridiculous. – Jen

June is more accepting of the belief that clothing does affect whether women are sexually harassed in public. Although making the point that she does not dress in order to get catcalls, she still feels it is her appearance that is the cause of men's actions, that certain types of clothing can "engineer" a response.

> It depends on some very outward signals, so like when I was at university I used to go around in just like baggy trousers and a top or whatever, baggy hoodie, and never had any hassle at all. When I got home and I was going somewhere and I was wearing quite a short skirt, I got two wolf whistles on the walk to the bus stop from my house which is like a 10-minute journey after like two months of no one saying anything at all. It just reminds you that it's almost like they're reacting to signals, or like you can kind of engineer it, not that I was going out wearing a short skirt so I would get catcalls.

Marly and Lisa shared a similar sentiment, speaking about the need to incorporate harassment into an outfit choice in order to lessen the emotional impact of being catcalled. Describing it as an unwanted yet inevitable consequence of dressing in a particular way.

> In terms of my everyday outfit which is basically black jeans always, flat shoes, I don't get anything in this. I feel comfortable in this, I can't remember any situation where it's happened at all. But when I'm wearing high heels and a short skirt I get looks a lot and I might get other stuff. I wish none of it would happen but I guess I've come to a point where it's inevitable, it's going to happen, almost to the extent where it's like, 'Ok I'm going to wear this so I know it's going to happen', so it becomes part of the outfit. – Marly

> That's what makes me really angry is that if I choose to wear big boots and a short skirt that will draw

comments. And the thing is when I wore that outfit I wasn't that surprised when someone wolf-whistled when I walked past. It was like, 'Oh yeah of course, I was kind of expecting that.' And it wasn't that I could just wear that and go out. And I guess that's why that time it didn't really annoy me that much because I was kind of expecting it. – Lisa

Like understanding men's actions as complimentary, if we can engineer and expect it we are in control. What lies underneath this, however, is a form of unspoken 'common sense': if you dress like that you have to expect men's intrusion. If it goes too far, you've only got yourself to blame. The problem, again, is an individual one. The problem, again, is you.

Jacqueline gave a particularly powerful example of this through an account of how intrusion from unknown men acted as a trigger for her ex-husband's violence against her. Believing her appearance was the reason for this attention from male strangers, Jacqueline tried to change the way she looked.

If I was out with him, in public, and another man looked at me and I happened to be looking up at the time he would take me around the corner somewhere and do something bad to me. And then when we got home he would beat me to different degrees. It made me physically cut my hair, stop wearing make-up, never wear a skirt, cover up, eventually not wear perfume and not wear jewellery. I didn't ask for this attention, yet it was my fault, he said it was my fault.

The judgement from Jacqueline's ex-husband that it was her fault was unchallenged by a society that locates women as the cause of men's actions. The change only came years later when he almost killed her and, after being in hospital for weeks, Jacqueline found a space to leave. She was only then free to talk about experiences she'd had with unknown men in public.

And I've told friends that and they've gone, 'Oh that happened to me'. But I didn't know that happened to people. When it happened to me I thought this is just me and it's my fault because maybe I didn't have my hair cut or put too much make-up on or whatever. I think society lets people down in a way doesn't it?

Like Jacqueline's belief that long hair and make-up were to blame for intrusion by unknown men and the subsequent violence from her husband, the trimmings associated with a feminine appearance were repeatedly mentioned as those that were unsafe, either always or in particular contexts such as being alone or at night. For some women, then, avoiding these markers becomes tied to an attempt to disappear completely.

Reducing

Gail, Becky and Bea, a White British woman in her mid-twenties, all spoke about trying to reduce how conventionally feminine they looked in public.

> I'd tie my hair up for some reason, I'd think if I tied my hair up and scowled I just wouldn't look like anyone someone would want to talk to. I'd just try to look like I didn't want anyone to talk to me. I think it's quite easy to disappear. – Gail

> I'd wear tights and a longer skirt, I think you get a massive difference in reaction if you wear heels so I'll take flat shoes with me or, I quite like to wear red lipstick but if I'm going home by myself I'll take that off sometimes because it gets too much attention because people will look at you and think she must be up for it. – Becky

> It's mainly for me just that having to think about what you wear when you go out. Like if I'm going to get the night bus, it sounds so extreme, but I won't go out wearing a dress, I'll wear jeans just because it's safer and in the back of your mind you're probably thinking at least I can run away if I don't wear a skirt

and high heels, don't wear a low cut top, wear a scarf just in case you need to wrap it around. It sounds so extreme and it's not something that's at the forefront of your mind, but it's always there. – Bea

The fact that the accessories and attributes that are understood as causing harassment, from long hair to jewellery, red dresses and lipstick, are those that we mostly associate with only women – that in essence what we are saying is that *womanhood is unsafe* – is left wholly unexamined. And yet this underlying message has implications not only for evaluating clothes in terms of safety, but in terms of a feeling of unsafety in a female body. Delilah and Nisha, for example, told me how they had used clothing to reduce the visible markers of womanhood. For Delilah it was about trying to take attention away from her body, particularly her breasts, while Nisha found a way to use make-up as a mask to protect her.

I dress with scarves and things to just cover, take the focus away from my breasts … also I now stay away from the colour red ever since I wore red one day and everyone just kept commenting, 'Oh you with the tight red dress'. And I just thought it's not necessarily tight, it's knee length, it's got shoulders, it's not a provocative dress, but because it was *red* red and you should be a wallflower basically. So I steer clear of red which is such a shame because I love it, so I wear hot pink or burgundy, things that are similar to red but I always think a bit, ooo, think twice about wearing red. Yeah. I never really think that much about it but it does affect the way you carry yourself. – Delilah

When I was in my younger teens, up to about 14, I started to wear like really Gothy clothes, used to wear a lot of black, a lot of eyeliner, and lots of chains and stuff, but I think in a way some of that might have warded some of that attention off a little bit. And I think that's part of the reason why I did it. Because I felt sexualised from a really early age and I didn't

> want to feel like that. My mum used to say to me, 'Oh
> you're wearing a mask'. And I think I was, because
> I was trying to cover myself up literally with all this
> make-up and these clothes and whatever and I think
> to a certain level that did stop it from happening as
> much. – Nisha

Again we see that feeling less visible as a woman equates with feeling safer – as Gail said earlier, the goal seems to be to disappear. But for some women this isn't possible. Markers of race, class, sexuality and disability can mean that sometimes the safety of invisibility is unavailable. Marly addresses these limits below, connecting to Josina's experiences in Chapter Two. Both women spoke about how having a female partner meant their relationship felt visible in a way not experienced by heterosexual women, purely for the ways in which heterosexuality is unseen.

> I've been followed by a guy once but that's probably
> because I was with another girl at the time and we
> were kissing in the streets and this guy had seen us
> in the nightclub and he decided to follow us home.
> And in the end we started running and he came
> banging on our front door, so we closed it. That
> was quite scary, even though I wasn't alone. The
> intersections with guys about misogyny and sexism
> and guys about gay stuff.

This has also been shown in the work of two of the UK's leading women's organisations: Imkaan, a specialist organisation for groups working to end violence against women of colour; and the End Violence Against Women Coalition (EVAW), a coalition of over 80 groups and individuals working on violence against women throughout the UK.[11] In 2016, Imkaan's young women's team Purple Drum and EVAW created a short film to highlight the ways in which public sexual harassment is racialised for young women from black and minoritised ethnic groups – many of whom are visible in ways they are unable to escape, such as through their skin colour or religious dress.[12] In 2018, Purple Drum followed this up with another film using the testimonies of young queer women of colour to demonstrate how not just gender and race can affect a women's visibility, but also sexuality as shown by Marly and Josina, and, importantly, age. While age can make it harder for younger women to disappear, for women who are older it can mean that invisibility is experienced but not necessarily desired. Both Clare and Ruth describe their experience of ageing as feeling caught in a contradiction.

> So I feel that recently as I get into my early forties and I think about my fifties and I worry about being invisible, I feel this unsolvable dichotomy between dressing attractively and passivity. So I feel that when I put attractive clothes on that I become passive, sexually vulnerable and that my brain just isn't important in the dialogue and also that the discomfort, the physical discomfort, stops me thinking. So I walk through the streets and feel that I advertise that I've given up. It's just an uneasy, unresolved issue. It's if I dress up I feel vulnerable, if I don't dress up I feel daggy and unattractive. Most of the time I'll settle for the daggy and unattractive, but the male gaze is always there. – Clare

> I'm not saying it never ever happens to me but about it being an everyday thing, I don't know if it is for me. I'm sure that it does go on, but I walk around completely unaware of it. So I was kind of just interested in, 'Ok well let's try to be interested in it and just see'. And I've tried to be more aware of it, and nothing's happened so I feel conflicted. I don't feel like I'm old enough to be invisible, not yet. – Ruth

Because interruption from unknown men is often framed as not just complimentary and inevitable but fundamentally about *being* a woman, to not receive this kind of behaviour can be experienced as a lack, an embarrassment, again as if the problem is us. Carolyn learnt this after talking to a group of younger women and older women about being shouted at in the street.

The other girls in my group, some of whom were a bit younger, one of whom was about my age, said they liked being catcalled and they felt bad if it didn't happen to them. And I just thought that was awful that they're, it really made me angry that they're growing up and they think that that's a good thing to be an object. But then I was talking to my auntie and my mum about it and they said that when they got just over 50 it just stops and they become invisible. And that makes them freaked out. Because then what are they?

Men's intrusion becomes so much a part of being a woman that without it we are made to feel we might not be anything at all. This starts to expose the double bind: the need for women to walk a tightrope between invisibility, attractiveness, and asking for it. For Anna it is about the ways in which women's space is closed down, bordered on either side by competing demands.

Women should be able to feel really confident about the way that they look and who they are you know and take their space but it's this constant, when you do that it's not ok to do that. It's a bit like, 'Well who do you think you are?' Yes, we want you to look beautiful and glamorous and attractive to us and as soon as you are we'll push you down again because it's too threatening, too intimidating for us.

This conflict reveals the ways in which men's intrusion, and the messages directed at women about it, impacts more than women's actions. Avoidance and self-protective behaviours such as changing movements and clothing limit women's freedom to act in ways they choose without fear of violence or harassment. However, there is something even deeper than this going on. Talking to women about their experiences in public reveals how much safety work is about a reduction. Anna discusses her consciousness of this in talking about being confronted with men creating a sexually threatening environment.

Because I am a tall woman and I want to be proud of my height I don't want to walk around with a stoop, and I do often wear heels because I like to be tall and I like my height and I'm proud of it and I don't close myself off and I think that definitely does give that message that you're open and you're available. But in that kind of environment I was talking about with those men, the effect that would have would be to immediately make me, make my posture change and I would look down and be more sort of covered in the way that I walked.

Her response is connected to that desire to dress in ways where we can disappear. Here, instead of clothing, the change is made to women's bodies themselves, to how they are in the world, in order to be smaller, less visible. Like the difference between safety from and to, the limitation here is on our ability to *be*.

Being

When Gail finished her A Levels, she went inter-railing through Europe for two weeks. Even though she was only 17, she had pre-planned the whole thing with her mum and so she felt really organised and excited to travel alone. What she found out pretty quickly was what it was like being a woman in public.

Every single day some guy would talk to me and I found it really annoying. I think because I was blindingly white compared to everyone else, and really young. But there was this tactic that I noticed where they'd just come up and say hello and I'd say, 'Hello' and then they'd say, 'How old are you?' Or, 'Where are you from?' And it'd always be questions so you wouldn't just say no, they wouldn't say, 'Do you want to talk?' They'd just keep asking these little questions where you'd think this isn't intrusive, this is just friendly questions and you feel like you should answer and then it would become increasingly more uncomfortable so, it'd move to like, 'Oh can we write maybe, you give me your address?' and I'd be like, 'How about you give me your address?' Just kind of spending part of my day each day just trying to get out of conversations I didn't want to have. Every day.

Particularly interesting given her earlier comments on the ease of disappearing, Gail here talks about the impossibility of her doing just this. Taken out of a context where her racialisation is invisible, Gail is made conspicuous through characteristics she cannot control or hide. After this experience of frequent interruption by unknown men in public, she had an incident with a man in a hostel that made her decide to change herself.

At this youth hostel this guy started talking to me in the laundry and I was like, oh this is really nice, he's just another friendly traveller. And then he went to shake my hand, and I was like, oh ok. And then he went to kiss my hand, and I thought, oh, oh ok. And then he put my finger in his mouth and I thought, what the hell are you doing? No. Like this is, what the hell? And I stormed out and then, luckily, after that I went and put my sunglasses on and my earphones in and it was like the best cure I'd ever discovered to being able to walk around without anybody being able to talk to me.

The 'cure' Gail finds then is a way of disappearing into yourself when you cannot disappear from the world, to block off or segment yourself from your surroundings. Alongside a change to movements and clothing, some women try to find a way of being in the world without being wholly present, where to be present as a woman in public is to be vulnerable. One of the most obvious ways of doing this is through finding some kind of barrier, like the sunglasses and headphones adopted by Gail. These create a separation, or simply *the illusion* of a separation, both of which can help women to feel safer, as described by Hannah below.

One of the strategies I've developed is I'll always be listening to music. So I can pretend I haven't heard someone. And I only realised this recently when I started thinking about it. It is a defence thing because if someone's saying something and I'm ignoring them and they think I can't hear them and start calling me a bitch or whatever, I can't hear them saying that so it doesn't matter to me because all I can see is their facial expression and that doesn't really bother me. It's only really what they're saying that really upsets you. So they can say whatever they like because if I'm got my music in I can't hear them so that's fine. Make it louder. Then when I got into town and was walking anywhere I'd turn it off, but have my headphones in, because then if anything happened I could either ignore it or pretend I hadn't heard it. Which is probably what other people do but I thought it was something I just did.

This is not to claim that the use of such accessories is limited to women or that it is always about creating safety through distance. Sunglasses and headphones, like being distracted by a phone or choosing to sit somewhere a bit away from people on public transport, are also ways that people in general try to create a sense of their own private space in public. But what we see in the accounts of Gail and Hannah is the way in which this distancing can serve a particular purpose for women wanting to put some space between themselves and a world that feels unsafe. For Jan, this speaks to how women are encouraged not only to want to separate from being in the world, but from being in their bodies, something the philosopher Simone de Beauvoir terms bodily alienation.[13]

They're not at home in their bodies. They're outside of their bodies because their body has always been criticised and so much happens to young women's bodies they're not ok just by themselves. It's not there for them to live in really. It's a catch-22. There's no space there. I mean I carried quite a lot of weight for quite a lot of my life, I think that was a bit of a protection really. Because I've got a very curvaceous figure and people tend to be like, 'Oh my God!' And I don't really want to be like that, I want to choose when I want to do that stuff. It's only really in the last few years I would wear something this fitting, and it's like, it's my body, it's ok you know, if I want to wear something fitting that shows my shape, I can. I now feel I can protect myself in other ways, I don't have to carry a sheath around me of clothes, there was quite a lot of that.

More than just a comment on the ways in which she, like many women, used clothing or accessories as a form of protection, in saying "there's no space there", Jan is revealing the ways in which repeated exposure to both men's actions and the messages given about them, changes women's ways of being, both in the world and in themselves. Clare, who spoke in the previous section about the tension between wanting to be invisible and wanting to be attractive, understands the impact of this in a similar way to Jan: resulting in a sense of unbelonging in her own body.

> In between the good/bad dichotomy you get these crossovers where you get good equals also being attractive in the right way but not too much. So you're walking this tightrope of balance. Am I dressing up in a way where I'm being sexually provocative or am I dressing up in a way that's attractive? What can I get away with? And what would make me feel comfortable is lost. So there's no comfort in one's sexuality. There's no comfort in being in one's body.

This idea of bodily discomfort relates closely to the ways in which both Taryn, a White Australian in her late thirties, and Rosalyn, a White British woman in her late twenties, talked about the relationship between their body and invisibility.

> Actually when I was younger I lost a lot of weight. How I deal with stress is I lose weight and once I got

onto drugs and lost a shitload of weight, I was really thin, like a small size 8 which is really tiny for me. And I actually physically became invisible. I got no male attention. And I was quite young too so it was actually at the height of male attention, young and heterosexual, and I actually really liked it, because I felt invisible. – Taryn

There's another bit of me that also wishes, because having a skinny boyish figure means you can wear certain types of clothes and we're all supposed to want to be like that, but I think there's a bit of me that wishes that because, I guess because you feel like it's a kind of less conspicuous sexuality about that kind of body on a woman. – Rosalyn

Here the pleasure of invisibility is connected not just to having less womanly accessories, as seen in the discussion of clothing, or to being less connected to the world, as seen through the use of distancing strategies. What both Taryn and Rosalyn are talking about here is a safety in having less of a woman's body. If a woman's body is unsafe in the world, and the risk is understood as not only being in the world, but in the body itself, then reducing the risk means reducing the body. This is seen in its most obvious sense in Sophie's retelling of a conversation she had with a friend who had very large breasts and decided to get a breast reduction, something that in her words made her "beautifully invisible".

I was talking to her about the fact that I was going to come and see you and I said you know, 'What was it like before?' and she said, 'People used to look at my boobs and be like, "Look at the tits on that"'. And she said, 'That's exactly how it used to make me feel, like a that, not a person. I'm a thing, I'm two walking boobs on legs'. And I asked her how she felt when she had this boob reduction, and she used the phrase 'beautifully invisible'. Which really upset me because she's amazing and why should she have to want to be invisible? It just made me sad.

However, as seen in the previous section, it is not just in terms of a physical reduction that women are made to feel like they should be smaller. Rosalyn helps to make sense of this in explaining further her feeling of being conspicuous.

> I become really aware of my body I think, and I feel bigger and more conspicuous. If I'm wearing things like a dress that makes me feel more vulnerable. I do think what I wear might make a difference, definitely the clothes that I wear do make a difference, but then I'm not sure whether that's my perception because it makes a difference in various different ways. It can make a difference to the amount of interactions with male strangers I have and that's something that I feel is true but there's a bit of me that thinks, you just think that's true, because it makes a difference to how I *feel* when those things happen. Like I definitely feel if I've got a dress on or if I'm wearing a short skirt then there's a vulnerability in feeling consciousness and conspicuousness about my body, that's what I feel like. And that's what I mean about feeling bigger.

The commonality of this feeling of bodily self-consciousness becomes particularly evident in looking at women's accounts of what goes on for them when they feel they're being stared at. The similarities are clear in the descriptions from June, Viola and Abbey about what happens internally as they pass groups of men.

> I feel uncomfortable walking past them because I feel there's a chance they will say something if that makes sense. I become very conscious of the fact that I don't really know here to look, and we get back to the whole either looking at the ground or looking straight ahead thing, and I find myself trying to think of what a normal person would do who wasn't feeling self-conscious. – June

You can feel your heart rate going up a bit and then you're really conscious of the way you're walking and then your walk gets funny because you're really conscious about it. It's rubbish. And part of me thinks no, this isn't right; ok, you're looking at me, I can look at you. But then I don't, I don't quite feel able to. – Viola

I feel like I'm on a catwalk as I walk by because they're all lined up and I'm walking by, and I notice them from far away and I start to become really conscious of how I'm walking and what I'm wearing and how I'm looking as I'm approaching them and as I'm walking by. And try really hard not to look at any of them. Even though I'm hypersensitive of the fact they are there I try to act like they're not. – Abbey

For all three women it is not only that the body becomes in Rosalyn's words "bigger" or more obvious, but that women's relationship to it changes. This over-awareness of our bodies is what Jan is talking about in relation to an inability for young women to live in their body; to feel safe and at home, at *ease*. Katie-Lou touches on something similar in relation to how she feels disorientated when men interrupt her in public.

I feel disorientated a bit, and kind of scrutinised. Because obviously I'm doing something, I'm going somewhere I'm doing something specific and they interrupt what I'm doing. I feel off kilter a little bit, obviously uncomfortable, but it kind of leaves me feeling stupid as well because I don't know what the right reaction is, I don't know what they expect of me. I feel like I'm knocked off balance a little bit. If they take me by surprise then obviously I've not got my phone out so I can't do my usual distracting technique, so then I kind of scurry off but feel a little bit small, feel a bit stupid.

Feeling too big through being conscious of the possibility of harassment, or made small by experiences we weren't able to predict, what we are seeing are some of the ways that women have been trained to literally take up less space. A training that provides the perfect counterpoint to behaviours such as 'manspreading', where men take up more than their allotted space, generally on public transport.[14] Both physically and symbolically such practices limit the space available for women, requiring us to reduce ourselves. No wonder our relationship to our bodies becomes one of control rather than care. Similar to Jacqueline commenting earlier in this chapter about feeling like sexual harassment from unknown men had made it easier for her ex-husband to abuse her, here we see its role in the relationship we have with our body. For many women, at some point in our lives, this relationship is marked by distrust or dislike. Without negating the part played by the beauty, diet, and fashion industries, the impact of sexual harassment needs to be addressed in discussions about the factors contributing to negative body image in women. What we find is that a hidden form of safety work is this bodily alienation, to view our body as not us but a thing to control and use. We learn to reduce ourselves – physically, symbolically – to burrow down deep inside our body as a way to feel safer.

Having explored the context behind safety work and its content, now we start to see its consequence. Rather than being the expression of ourselves in the world, what allows us to walk past, to look and speak back, our body becomes alien to us, separate. Like the wall Theodora spoke about putting up in Chapter Three, we become trapped inside, outside, or behind it. Our body becomes just another thing in the world rather than *being us in the world*. And so, alienated from our bodies and separated from our world, taught to doubt ourselves yet blamed if anything happens, reducing ourselves, restricting our space, this is the setting within which women find themselves trapped; tasked with deciphering the right amount of panic.

FIVE

The right amount of panic

Force of habit

The philosopher Maurice Merleau-Ponty wrote a lot about habit, in particular something that he called the habit body. For Merleau-Ponty, habit is the way we make the world, *our* world. It shows how we can absorb new meanings, demonstrating that we have 'assimilated a fresh core of significance',[1] about ourselves and our surroundings. He believed that some habits are not stored in thought or even really in the physical body; they are only revealed in how we interact with our environment. Think about the way we can leave the house unsure if we shut all the windows or turned off the oven. On returning to double check we see that we did do these things but without a conscious awareness. Our bodies complete the task while our minds are elsewhere, already thinking about where we are going or what we need to do when we get there. This is part of what he is saying but it isn't the whole story. If you needed to consciously shut the windows or turn off the oven you would 'know how' to do it, this know-how is stored in your conscious mind even though the tasks can be performed without it. But some habits are captured in the body itself, or more specifically in the way the body interacts with the world. Through this they can be hidden from view, only revealed when they are disrupted.

I recently learnt this in a fairly embarrassing way on trying to type the PIN for my bankcard into a machine where the numbers weren't in their usual place. My fingers habitually flew to where they usually went but when I realised the keypad was different, I couldn't actually remember what the individual numbers were. Even trying to imagine a key pad didn't work; I had to physically draw the usual keypad and let my fingers do their thing, to be able to pay for breakfast. The ways in which my PIN was embodied, revealed only through my interaction with the world, is what Merleau-Ponty means by the habit body. What Theodora and Cathy alert us to below are the ways in which this may operate in relation to women's safety work.

When Theodora was 15 she had a man masturbate at her on public transport, a different one than the man she mentioned in Chapter Three who masturbated at her on the District line – it really *is* that common. This time she was on a bus, in the seat closest to the window, and the man beside her just started "jerking off". Being scared and young, Theodora waited until her stop, and then politely asked to get past him which he politely allowed her to do. But the impact of what he did that day didn't end when she got off the bus. It gave her a particular message about what is and isn't safe, a message she stills draws on over ten years later.

> I was sitting on the bus, on the inside seat which is something I quickly learnt never to do if I can find another seat available. I don't do it anymore. Oh no, I would never now get onto a bus and sit by the window. I do that really annoying thing which everyone hates where I sit on the edge even though there's a seat right there and then if someone comes to sit next to me I'll stand up and let them sit in, in particular if it's a guy. Actually maybe not even in particular if it's a guy. If it's someone who's bigger than me, I'll let them go inside because then I figure at least I can get away.

Cathy's experience on the bus as a child, recounted in Chapter Three, resulted in something similar, an adaptation of the meaning of safety. For Cathy, however, the threat is not the inside seat, it is any empty seat beside her.

> What happened was after that I think I had a term of riding home on the bus because my mum stopped

> working so she was at home and I just got the bus for half a term until we moved away. And I was terrified getting on the bus so what I did was if I'd see a lady on her own, I'd wait for the bus to start moving and I'd get a place but as soon as it started moving and I saw someone appropriate to sit next to I'd go sit next to them, so the bus was moving and then this old biddy would be like, 'What the hell are you doing?'

Though here both women remember the exact experience that caused a change, this is not always or perhaps even often the case. Habit is not simply a mechanical response to external or internal stimulus but rather it is a form of embedded practical understanding. In responding to future situations through what we've learnt from those that came before, we take on what is called an embodied principle. Rather than continually experiencing the world anew, we are able to transform the unknown into a familiar context and identify an appropriate response through this use of embodied principles. These courses of action repeated over time come to form habits; particular ways we *are* in the world.[2] This can be seen in Laura's approach to choosing seating on public transport. She finds safety in the space that Cathy finds frightening, showing that, for women in public, what safety means is not set or certain.

> Usually when I get on a bus you go for the area that feels safest. I usually go upstairs, I guess, I don't know, I think you can see more there. And then I'll sit somewhere where there's a good space around me. So if there's three sets of seats that aren't occupied I'll sit in the middle one so there's space around me. But I guess most people do that anyway don't they? Try to get as much personal space as possible?

As Laura's decisions about where to sit aren't directly connected to an experience she can remember, seeking space like this is framed as common sense. But in reading the accounts of Theodora and Cathy we see that what safety looks like might not be so common after all. Thinking back to Chapter Four where Cathrin spoke about being told off by her friends for walking home alone at night, or Clare shared her involuntary judgements of women in heels, this understanding can start to challenge some of the ways we may inadvertently blame others and ourselves. What safety looks like is different for different women, based on our own embodied principles, though the fact that we have had to consider what it looks like *at all* is a shared reality.

Over time these individual changes, often made in response to the actions of men, can hide themselves in our habits and we can forget why we started doing them in the first place. Claire gives a striking example of this. She told me about how she used to walk through a large common near her house late at night, something she decided to change.

> I think that I was probably a bit more naïve then in a way, or brave. I don't know, those are completely the wrong words to be using as well because why shouldn't I be walking through there at three in the morning? There's nothing wrong with that, that's my way home. Why should I have to go all the way around the houses? I really don't know what it was that changed, there was no incident or anything like that. I think it was just slowly thinking I need to change my behaviours, I don't remember a determining factor where it was like, 'Right that's it now' or anything that happened to a friend or anything like that. I think it's just, I don't know.

Look at how Claire frames this; no determining factor, no reason. Just a change in how naïve I was. How brave I was. My own decision. Except that after speaking for another 20 minutes or so, Claire started to remember that there was a reason. That it wasn't about her, but about an incident with a male stranger.

> There was this thing that did give me a bit of a jolt in terms of maybe I shouldn't be doing this. So yeah actually thinking about it after saying nothing happened, actually something did happen where I

was walking through the common at about 10.30pm and it was dark and I was aware that someone was walking at the same pace but slightly behind me. And I had to cross this road so I stopped and he stopped and he asked me what time it was and I said, 'I don't know I haven't got the time' because I was aware that if I looked down he could have done something, so I just said, 'No, no I don't have the time, sorry.'

Claire was just about to set off again when the man tried another time to get her attention, calling after her repeatedly, "excuse me, excuse me". She thought that he'd already had a chance to ask her something legitimately so didn't stop this time and quickly began to cross the road.

And I think just as he started to follow me a car came and it meant that he couldn't follow me so I went even quicker down the road. And there was something in that that made me think this is really silly, there's no one around and it's pitch black and it's so badly lit on the common that I can't keep walking through here.

The actions of the man who followed her at night through a park are hidden, with the way it made her limit her movements remembered only as her decision. However, agency – the capacity to act within a space – is not the same as freedom – the ability to define the space for action.[3] Like Theodora sitting on the outside seat, Claire's actions here do not originate in her. Neither paranoid or irrational, they are a strategic response to the actions of intrusive men; designed to decrease the possibility of escalation. Routine and repeated, this limitation becomes habit, and what happened to make her adapt in the first place is filed away. This is how the process of habituation can reconstruct women's safety work as an act of choice – like the #homesafeselfie – making it harder for us to see the full consequences of men's intrusive practices. This process means that unearthing our safety work is not only about acknowledging the things we know we do: the headphones, crossing the road, bringing a scarf. Or even the ways we change how we are in public: taking up less space, bag on our lap, looking at the ground. As started to be shown at the end of the last chapter, understanding the full extent of women's safety work involves unpacking the habits that have been stored in the body.

Hannah describes the workings of this in relation to the first time she experienced any form of intrusion. At 16, Hannah was walking home from work down a main road. A car pulled up next to her with two men in their early twenties, asking for directions to the local college:

> So I gave them the directions, they listened to me and everything, and then at the end of it the guy on the passenger side said, 'Has anyone ever told you you're pretty?' And I really didn't know what to say so I think I just went, 'no'. Because that was just my gut reaction to say no. And then can't remember exactly what he said next but ultimately he said, 'Give us a blow job'. And then made a lewd gesture. I was just shocked. I had absolutely no idea why anyone would say that to somebody. And like I say because it was my first experience of that I just couldn't believe that someone had said it to me.

Despite how shocked she was, despite the fact it didn't make sense, Hannah already understood not to talk about it. By 16, she already knew.

> I don't think I told anybody. I don't remember because nowadays on Twitter and things like that I would say something. But when I was 16 I didn't have access to any of that and I wouldn't have wanted to say anything to my parents because I wouldn't have wanted to worry them that people were saying stuff like that to me in the street. I just don't think I mentioned it to anyone. Which looking back on it is really strange because it would have been a really odd thing that happened to me. It's like you've tried to rationalise it in your head, you've gone through

the process and then it's just filed away in your brain somewhere. Only for you to discover years later that it happened.

When we truly grasp the force of habit we realise that there's a lot we might not think we remember, but our body has captured its meaning. These experiences aren't necessarily filed in our conscious minds all the time. Instead, like my PIN, the learning is written into how we are in the world in a way that only reveals itself through action. We learn not to store the specifics – of our stories, those of others, or wider representations – but rather to keep the lessons about risk, and how we should adapt. Once this has happened we can forget what caused it all and reconfigure what we do as a result as choice or common sense. Not having to hand the experiences that informed our decisions in the first place can feed that feeling we are paranoid or that we've got it wrong – again the irrational woman. We find it is not only our work that is made invisible but also the actions of men.

The escalation calculation

During her work with young women who had been in local authority care, the sociologist Maddy Coy drew on Merleau-Ponty's work on the habit body to develop something she called an experiential template of risk.[4] She used this idea to talk about the ways in which the care system, together with experiences of sexual violence and childhood neglect, can encourage particular habits in the body, leading, for example, to an ease with distancing strategies that can be drawn on in the commercial exchange of sex. It's a useful concept when trying to think about how the habits we hold in our bodies influence our future actions, something we need to do if we are to fully understand the operations of women's safety work.

Many women in public space respond to the environment and unknown men using an escalation calculation, drawing on a template of risk to evaluate the safest course of action. This evaluation includes not only an evaluation of the man himself, but of the entire situation – including whether other people would intervene should the men's actions escalate – as Cathrin's account shows.

> I can be sassy and bantery and control it in that way but it could go wrong, they could get aggressive and angry and it could all go wrong so just in case, I'll look to see if somebody's sitting over there and I hope he has the courage to stand up or I'm going to call him out because he or she can't hide. So it's considering the level of engagement and counterbalancing this with the fight or flight response. What am I going to do?

Here, Cathrin's difficulty in deciding whether to challenge men or ignore them is rooted in evaluating the possibility of escalation and the knowledge that should this happen, she will be responsible for provoking rather than preventing it. Rosie spoke about a time where, in her words, it did "go wrong" and responding to a man's intrusion resulted in the most violent experience of harassment she'd ever had.

> This one time it was literally probably about ten feet away from my front door. I was walking down the road and I don't live on a very busy street so there was nobody around but it was daylight you know, it wasn't dark or anything. And this guy was just by his car and I can't for the life of me remember what he said but he whispered or murmured something under his breath, like, 'alright darling'. And I frequently now retaliate because I just can't stand by and let this happen, so I was like, 'Oh excuse me did you say something to me?' And then he looked really taken aback and was just like sheepishly, 'Oh, yeah, just said alright darling' or something, and I said, 'Look you just can't speak to anybody like this. It's sexist. It's street harassment. You don't realise how often this happens, it's completely inappropriate.' And then he said, 'Oh you're such a frigid cunt.' And then I had a massive go at him and he got really angry and I

retreated into my house. But then I realised that could have been really dangerous, he could have forced his way in as I opened the front door. It really shook me up, I've never had a response like that before. Just so, so violent.

As Rosie's account shows, the calculation doesn't always end at the end of the encounter. It can continue after initial action is taken, assessing the consequences, adjusting our response. It looks forward to the future, drawing on lessons from the past, to establish how to act in the present. Jane describes this through talking about an experience when she was in her flat alone at night with the curtains open, and on looking up realised that there was a man standing in the window of the building opposite who had been staring directly at her as she was moving around her flat.

> So I freeze and I pick up my phone and call my boyfriend and immediately he sees I'm on the phone. He must have been there for about 15 minutes, immediately he sees I'm on the phone he leaves and turns off the lights. And then of course I put the blinds down. And so again you know I can't do anything because (a) he didn't do anything and (b) if I did complain he knows which flat I'm in, he works across the street from my building all night, seven till seven. And if I complained about creepy behaviour it might set him off more. So I can't do anything.

In calling her boyfriend, Jane changed the man's actions, made him turn off the light and leave, and yet she discounts this in feeling like she cannot do anything. She feels stuck even though what she did worked.

The desire to prevent escalation, however, is complicated by the fact that sometimes it is only such escalation that will confirm what is, or isn't, happening. As seen in Chapter Three, women are taught to doubt their own sense-making of an experience and this can be particularly difficult when men use ambiguous spaces to intrude – is he pressing into me on the tube or is it just overcrowding? Is he following me or maybe going the same way? At times like these, the only way to know for certain is for the men's behaviour to escalate – the pressing to become rubbing, the following to continue when she crosses the street. Rosalyn describes the difficulty in this, trying to assess the right response without being able to know for sure exactly what a stranger is doing.

> I was in the British Museum and I was meeting a friend but I had an hour beforehand so I went to look in one of their medieval rooms and I was just looking at things. And there's this guy next to me who was, well you know going around at the same pace as me, but it wasn't just that? Like that feeling when you know that he's looking at me as much as the stuff. And you're just waiting. And it went on and on and I couldn't do what I was doing. I was there to look at the stuff and I couldn't concentrate, because the whole time I was thinking, 'When are you going to talk to me? What are you going to say? What's the deal here?'
>
> I don't think I changed what I did, but it massively affected my ability to do what I was doing. Like you can't focus on the other thing that you were doing and also because you're constantly waiting for this thing to happen. And it makes you powerless as well because he hasn't done anything yet that you can object to, even knowing he will. It's that knowing and not knowing at the same time. You do know that something is going on but you don't have any actual, objective proof to turn around and say leave me alone because nothing's happened yet.

This idea of knowing and not knowing, like Charlie earlier saying she was "scared but not scared", shows the ways in which women are forced to take up ambiguous and sometimes contradictory positions in relation to harassment as a way of affirming their own reality. Eventually, this time, something did happen and Rosalyn felt able to respond. After following her around like this for a while, the man leaned over and asked if he could take her photograph.

> I just looked at him and said, 'No'. And then he said, 'I'm sorry I'm sorry' and ran out of the room. Which was a bizarre reaction but in a way it was a relief, just waiting for that moment where I could be like, 'No, leave me alone' and he did which was good. He didn't try and stay with me or anything so I could just do what I was doing again but it's only at that point I think that you really become angry as well because before that you're so focused on thinking, what's going on here? And feeling anxious I think until you reach that crisis point where they actually do speak to you.

Rosalyn's account shows the ways in which these hidden calculations, routinely performed without remark, disrupt women's ability to enjoy their time in public space. This is particularly concerning given that for many women, with caretaking responsibilities at home and the invisible work of organising, cleaning, running households, public space can be the only space they truly have to themselves. Needing to anticipate the actions of that man, Rosalyn's awareness is focused externally – one eye on escalation – rather than being able to fully immerse herself in the museum and in herself. And it is not only when faced with a harasser that women are needing to do this. As seen in Chapter Three, women learn that the majority of their safety work needs to be pre-emptive, conducted before anything happens. We saw the forms this can take in Chapter Four with women talking about changes to their movements, clothes, and being. The force of habit, however, means that where risk has been captured by the body, such evaluations can take place without our conscious awareness. As Viola says, it's ingrained in what we do.

> I guess the difficult bit about it is that it's so ingrained in everything you do that a lot of the time you aren't really aware that you're doing it. So there might be

times when you're very aware because you have to go somewhere that's a bit unsafe or do something that you're a bit uncomfortable with in public space but then on a day to day basis you do it as well without even thinking.

Again our work is made invisible through being naturalised as part of what it is to be a woman. Just as habit can reconstruct our work as invisible to ourselves, the ways in which these templates change between women can mean that our work is invisible to others. For Mia, this forms part of the reason that so much of our work is dismissed by men as an over-reaction.

They probably don't realise what kind of effect it has, it can have cumulatively or just on your day to have someone say something and make you angry. I think guys who, when you react, take the piss out of you for getting angry, I mean that makes it even worse but they must genuinely think that we're making a fuss over nothing. And that's just mind blowing, I mean I can't figure out how much more, what else we can say, what other perspectives can we give them to bring it home?

Though several women spoke about a lack of understanding or solidarity from male friends or partners, Josina gave a particularly remarkable example of being judged for her safety work by a male stranger.

One time I got on this bus and I sat down, and it was two stops later and I pressed the bell to get off, and the guy next to me, who I was sitting next to, he laughed and I looked at him like, not like, 'Please tell me what's on your mind' but like, 'What the fuck? What's wrong with you?' And then he said, 'Oh I'm sorry it's just quite funny that you, well why did you bother getting on the bus it was only two stops?' And I was getting off the bus but I wanted to say something so I said, 'Look you're not a woman travelling on your

own in the middle of the night. You've got no idea.'
And he apologised, he was clearly just a bit cocky
... I just thought you know I'm thinking so much in
detail about how to get home safely on my own and
you're judging me, you've got no idea.

Josina's decision to catch a bus, like the vast majority of safety
work, is pre-emptive; designed to prevent what might happen.
Just as Cathrin and Rosie discussed their strategising when
responding during harassment, similar skilful assessments of the
environment – and adaptations of the self within it – are taking
place in order to prevent being harassed at all. For Anne, this is
a process of reacting both to something that's happened many
times before and to something that's not happened yet.

If you get used to these things happening you're
going to judge other people and think that it's going
to happen, it's happened so many times before. So
you're reacting to something that's not happened yet.
You're trying to prepare for it. But it shouldn't be a
case of not being prepared for it. It should be people
not doing it. Because the only way to truly avoid it is
to not go out but it's not worth that kind of sacrifice.

Understanding how women have built a template of risk, from
ourselves, from others, from lessons about safety, shows that
this preparation is not baseless. Though acting in relation to a
particular incident that may not have yet happened, we have built
a model based on previous experience to help assess possibility.
Katie-Lou, Jen and Jeannine discovered this in considering how
anticipation and preparation meant that sometimes just seeing
male strangers changed their actions in public.

I was thinking about this as well. I'm kind of
programmed that if I walk through a group of men
I prepare myself by distracting myself. Things like I'll
take my phone out or pretend to be doing things that
mean that I don't have to look at them if that makes
sense? Because I don't want them to say stuff to me so

I figure if I look like I'm busy, they might not say stuff to me. But then also if they do say stuff to me, they can't see my reaction, because I don't want to give them the satisfaction of me interacting with them. So I take my phone out if I'm approaching them. I'm not saying that they'll necessarily do something, I'm not saying that all men do that, but some men do that and if I feel that there's men standing around that might do that then that's something that I feel I might do. – Katie-Lou

I tend to cross the roads when I get off the tube down to our house, it's quite suburban and at night it's reasonably quiet. I mean you do tend to pass one person on the road it's not completely dead, but at night if there's a guy I tend to cross over, which is horrible. I've spoken to my husband about this and he's said that he feels bad sometimes walking behind a woman on the pavement and he feels that he needs to move because she might feel uncomfortable. And I feel bad sometimes. I think, well I'm crossing the road and that guy might think, 'God what a bitch she thinks I'm going to do something' and you know half the time he's probably not doing anything but I don't know and I'd rather just not have to deal with it to be honest. So I just cross the road. – Jen

Where I used to walk home there used to be construction on both sides of the street, you could never avoid it. So it was when you turn into the street look which side has more men and choose the other one and then call somebody and I hate that's such a conscious decision too. Yeah I find myself calling someone quite a bit. It's like coping mechanisms that over time we've trained ourselves to do I think. – Jeannine

Trained over time how to cope and yet these changes create a problem. If this kind of safety work is successful, nothing happens; Katie-Lou does not get spoken to because she looks busy, Jen is ignored as she's on the other side of the road, and Jeannine, having assessed which side is safer, has her phone to her ear and gets by without comment. How then are we to know if nothing happened because we were right and prevented it, or nothing happened because we were wrong to begin with? Taught to doubt ourselves, we often need escalation to confirm our feelings on men's actions but this is the same escalation that our safety work is designed to prevent. This is how women are stuck, caught in a catch-22.

A catch-22

Jan used the term 'catch-22' in Chapter Four when she was talking about how women's bodies weren't there for them to live in, but the phrase captures more than this; it speaks to the very contradiction underpinning what women are expected to do. The term comes from Joseph Heller's novel of the same name, used to signify what is also called a double bind: when there is no escape from a situation because of mutually conflicting conditions. Heller's novel is one of the clearest, and funniest, demonstrations of the absurdity of war, and the catch of the title refers to the frustrated attempts of the central characters, members of the US army air force during World War Two, to be deemed mentally unfit to fly and thus excused from duty.

> There was only one catch and that was Catch-22, which specified that a concern for one's safety in the face of dangers that were real and immediate was the process of a rational mind. Orr was crazy and could be grounded. All he had to do was ask; and as soon as he did, he would no longer be crazy and would have to fly more missions. Orr would be crazy to fly more missions and sane if he didn't, but if he was sane he had to fly them. If he flew them he was crazy and didn't have to; but if he didn't want to he was sane and had to. Yossarian was moved very deeply by the absolute simplicity of this clause of Catch-22 and let out a respectful whistle.

"That's some catch, that Catch-22," he observed.

"It's the best there is," Doc Daneeka agreed.[5]

In essence, the catch is that although anyone deemed mentally unwell was not obliged to fly missions during the war, anyone who applied to stop flying on the basis of being mentally unfit was showing a rational concern for their safety and so was sane enough to fly. The logic is perfect and yet the outcome is absurd. And the right amount of panic works in a similar way. Women are blamed if they do not act to prevent sexual violence, but if they act and do prevent sexual violence they are paranoid for acting *because nothing happened*. What is revealed by examining the reasoning of safety work is that women are doomed to fail as the only times that we can measure are the times we get it wrong, as this example from Lucy shows:

> I left a club late at night and I was just going to go home and a taxi and I was sitting down and this guy was like, 'Are you alright?' And I said, 'Yeah I'm fine'. But thinking why are you asking me that? That's a bit dodgy, I'll carry on walking. And then this other guy just came out of the shadows of a doorway and just grabbed me, was just holding onto me and I was like, 'What are you doing?' I just didn't know what to do and was trying to be really indignant and going, 'Let go of me now' because I really didn't know how to react. But at that point I wasn't on edge so I feel like I should have been more ready, should have had my keys. And then I felt bad because he wouldn't let go of me, this really tall guy and the other guy who'd asked me if I was alright came running down the road and yelled, 'Let go of her now', so he let go of me and I ran away. But then I felt really bad because initially I'd thought the first guy was evil but he was actually just checking if I was ok.

This moment stands out for Lucy as a failure of her ability to assess risk and safety. Taught both to blame and doubt herself, she feels the problem is her, in how she made sense of what was happening, in a similar way to how women and girls blame themselves in the aftermath of sexual violence: made responsible for not preventing it at the same time as being unable to claim any amount of success for when they've done exactly this. For Viola this makes it difficult for women to act, as they are caught between what they may feel is safe and the ways they have been taught to doubt themselves.

> I think sometimes that can be really dangerous as well because people do have a tendency to talk themselves down a bit, like even when you know something isn't quite right because you want it to be right you'll be saying it's fine, don't over react, don't panic, but then maybe it isn't and you aren't prepared or you haven't done something that maybe could have protected you. So it's a very difficult line to tread, you don't know where you're at, at any given time.

The problem is that success is an absence of what might happen. As such, this absence can always be attributed to the fact that it was never going to happen at all. As Lucy's story above shows, sometimes this may indeed be the case – given the first man's later actions it seems his initial approach to Lucy was motivated by good intentions. But it is equally as likely, yet hardly ever considered, that sometimes, maybe many times, women are – without remark or recognition – preventing sexual violence. The feminist sociologists Sue Wise and Liz Stanley highlight this; the ways that our success is hidden from view.

> The amount that sexual harassment is thwarted is a social invisibility – we can't see that women have skilfully and successfully assessed and dealt with a complicated social situation because success here is an "absence" of a predicted outcome.[6]

Unsure of where they stand, trying to balance these conflicting conditions yet unable to know if they're getting it right, it is difficult for women to do anything other than change themselves and be silent. To speak about these changes, about those quick assessments of the environment, of men, is to risk being seen as hysterical. After all, nothing has really happened – yet – but maybe nothing was going to happen in the first place.

The ways in which this works is particularly clear in accounts about following. As Alice describes below, unless it escalates – the very thing safety work is designed to prevent – women are often unable to know for certain what is happening.

> I think there's an inherent feeling of fear that means I always feel if there's a man walking behind me, I'm aware of it. If I get off the bus then I'm very aware of who's gotten off with me and I probably would have clocked them on the bus anyway, thinking, 'Right so, did that guy get off?' And then I'm thinking, 'Right that guy did get off', and then I'm very aware of how far he is behind me.
>
> There are certain little tricks I tend to use like checking, not over my shoulder but checking directly to my right or to my left because I can see in my periphery how close somebody is. I use my shadow on the floor, if I'm on the street I can tell how close they are to me. I always say if I can't see their head then they're too close to me. That's when I'd be worried. I'm very aware of men around me. And it's more than being followed. I've been 'followed' by people in inverted commas, and then I've been followed by people. And it's hard to discern which one of those that person is intending on because you're not them. And the problem is that unless that in inverted commas 'following' ends in an instant where they talk to you or they touch you or they do whatever, you don't know.

Both Kirsten and Carolyn, had experiences as teenagers where initially ambiguous actions from a male stranger continued, even escalated, after they took preventative action. For Kirsten this happened at 14 on her way to a ballet class while for Carolyn it was at 15 or 16, heading home or to a friend's house in the evening. The ways in which this behaviour continued after both women changed what they were doing allowed them to know whether, as Alice says, it was 'following' or following.

> I was on my way to ballet class and this man was following me, and he was really drunk and then I started to run and he came running after me and then, by that time I'd reached the ballet hall and I started knocking on the door because it was locked and my ballet teacher opened it from the inside and she let me in. And then I started crying because I got really upset ... I got really scared when that happened, I was panicking I thought I was going to die or something, it was really bad. – Kirsten

> I was walking home from school, no it was the evening – maybe I was walking to my friend's house? – and very noticeably a van slowed down behind me and he peered out and looked me up and down and I just thought something bad was going to happen. So I saw where he was going to turn around and went and hid. He just went really slow and I hid. I was only across the road from my house so I went and hid in the porch bit and he didn't see me, but he drove back really slowly looking. – Carolyn

Carolyn's account particularly resonated with me as I had something very similar happen when I was 20. It was one of the bigger ones so I've never forgotten it, but I still don't feel certain anything happened at all. Walking to work at a bagel shop in East Vancouver very early in the morning, the streets were dark and as I turned the corner something made me look back. I realised that a car I had passed earlier, parked, was now driving slowly behind me with its lights off. I knew I was about to go through an area away from houses and people and so as though it were perfectly natural I walked straight up to the front door of the first house I saw and knocked. I don't know what made me do that, it was never something I'd done before, but somehow it felt like the only course of action. To pretend I'd reached my destination. I looked back from the doorstep and saw the car, still with its lights off, drive slowly past. No one answered my knock, it was pre-dawn after all, but as soon as I saw the car pass I hid down the side of the house. All this time thinking, I'm being stupid. All this time thinking, just in case. From where I was hidden I saw the car turn around, and the man inside, looking, drove back past slowly. And just like Carolyn, I saw him not see me. I waited a few minutes until I thought he'd gone and ran the rest of the way, terrified and still, this inescapable feeling, even as I ran, maybe I got it wrong. Designed to prevent what would prove I was right, I will never be sure if I was successful. Maybe he was, maybe he wasn't, I'll never know, as Bea's account shows.

> Me and my sister were getting the night bus home one night and we think quite similarly, and I was convinced this guy was looking over at us and he was. And then he happened to get off at the same bus stop as us and so we started walking, we hold hands and stand closer and that kind of stuff and I think I was more panicked than she was but she was like, 'Yep ok let's walk faster', and then he walked faster. I was convinced he was following us, so I said, 'Let's just run, let's run home it'll take five minutes', so we started running and I was wearing these strange shoes and I slipped over in the middle of the road. And this happened like two years ago but I really hurt my hip, I slipped over, went into like the half splits, ripped this ligament, had to call my dad, and the guy just walked straight on past so he wasn't, maybe he was, maybe he wasn't, you'll never know.

This all means that women are left unable to experience ourselves as capable agents, skilfully navigating public space and disrupting opportunities for crimes against us. Left with just the fear and the feeling we're probably being stupid. Left with just the blame any time we get it wrong. We have been taught to doubt ourselves for so long that we discount the possibility that our work may be working. And so, stuck, the only way forward is to make the changes to ourselves and what we want to do. Over time it just becomes a habit to trade our freedom for safety.

Trading freedom for safety

Back in Chapter Four, Ginger listed the ways she scanned public transport, sitting next to women if she could, sometimes skipping trains even if it made her late for something. She told me that these kinds of changes were easier than being treated as though she were over-reacting, using a Lithuanian phrase to visualise this: "blowing an elephant out of a fly".

> I just think that's one of the simplest and easiest things to do. You know if you feel threatened you could go to someone who works on the tube and say, 'I don't feel safe', but at the same time you have that feeling in your head that maybe you're wrong about this and then you'll be the crazy hysteric. And no one wants to be the crazy hysteric. And it might be that you're right, it might be that you're wrong, but the potential situation is that you're wrong about this, blowing an elephant out of a fly. I don't know if you have that expression but it's a common one back home. It's if you think that you're exaggerating everything and it's not nearly as bad as you think it is, it feels like you've done something wrong. And in theory you've done something right, you know you feel unsafe. It should be real, it should be reasonable enough for you to go to someone for help or go to someone to stop it but at the same time you also feel that well, apparently if it's not justified then people are going to look at me as one of those women.

What Ginger is describing here is the catch of the right amount of panic. Like the double bind seen across women's safety work – be attractive enough but not too much, cross the street, change trains, but don't be too obvious otherwise you'll attract their attention – women are carefully trying to balance their actions. But the trick is that there *can never be* a right amount of panic, there's only ever too much or not enough. With no way to know when we're getting it right, we're locked into giving up our freedom and being blamed regardless.

It is only in considering safety and freedom together that the true extent of our work is revealed, and yet the focus on safety in crime surveys and government policies, even sometimes in ourselves and in our judgements of other women, hides our ability to see this. Think back to Chapter Two and the typical questions used to measure fear of crime such as 'how safe do you feel walking in your neighbourhood at night?' No matter the answer to this, what we lose in the question is all of the work that women may be doing *to* feel safe: not wearing heels or the colour red, not taking a shortcut, scanning carriages, crossing the street, wearing headphones, looking down, playing with our phone, texting friends on the way. If we just focus on safety, as Sophie shows below, we lose the consequences of the quieter forms of intrusion – those that result in limiting women's freedom.

> Generally I feel quite safe actually. I think I've been quite lucky and I don't think from me you'll get like a shock story. I'm grateful for that don't get me wrong, there's no big story, but the thing that interested me about your study I think was that the low level, the small scale stuff that we put up with every day and just the deep impact it has on people. Like the fact I'm sitting here in this horrible black jumper when I'd really much rather be wearing something much more feminine. I do a lot of exercise and I eat well and I take care of my body and I have a really nice body I know that and yet I don't feel I'm able to dress it in a way I want to which sucks.

Not only is rape here a fortunate lack – I'm grateful there's no big story – but Sophie shows the ways that exploring women's safety work, from detail about what it looks like right through to how habit hides our work from ourselves, reveals women's freedom is in tension with their safety. In order to increase the latter, many women and girls routinely incorporate practices that limit the former, restrictions that are reconfigured as an act of choice. And it *is* a choice in a way, and that gives us an escape, because choices can be changed, as the final chapter will discuss. But the challenge is how to acknowledge this at the same time as recognising that choices are made in a particular context, one where we are responsible for preventing violence against us, one where we are blamed for failing. This kind of recognition is one we are rarely, if ever, encouraged to make.

The absence of a framework which acknowledges *both* that women have agency *and* that it is limited by the context in which it is exercised has been repeatedly shown in the context of child sexual exploitation. For example, a 2014 independent inquiry into child sexual exploitation in Rotherham, South Yorkshire, revealed systemic failings in the statutory response. Many of these were rooted in a misunderstanding of what appeared on the surface to be young women's agency, such as their exchanging sex for gifts or the affection of men who said they were their boyfriends.[7] The inquiry suggested a conservative estimate of approximately 1,400 children, most of these girls from white backgrounds aged between 11 and 16, were sexually exploited in this way from 1997 to 2013.[8] The sheer scale of offending only came to public attention through an investigation launched by *The Sunday Times* newspaper in 2011, which claimed that 'a repeated pattern of sexual offending existed in towns and cities across northern England and the Midlands involving groups of older men who groom and abuse vulnerable girls aged 11 to 16 after befriending them on the street'.[9]

Unlike known models of child sexual abuse, in which the vast majority of perpetrators are white men, this offending model was mostly perpetrated by men of Pakistani heritage, something that may be implicated in how widespread the media reporting was on it in comparison to the more familiar models of sexual abuse.[10] However, for our discussion it is the ways in which young women's agency was unable to be held here, alongside the existence of certain constraints that really stands out. Instead of being seen as making choices in a context of coercion and constraint, young women were imagined as free and entirely self-directed agents who were effectively choosing their own exploitation.

If we lose this link between restriction and action, seeing them as in opposition rather than in coalition, then unearthing and speaking about women's safety work risks reinforcing a similar message. This is important because although expanding the focus on safety to include its relationship to freedom gives a way of speaking back to common sense advice that focuses on actions women could take – never acknowledging those we do – the focus is still on the fact that women are changing themselves. Now, however, there's another reason to blame us: we become the reason for our own limitations. That this work may even be successful could be used to make women feel like they should do more – like some kind of safety work personal trainer: You've got this girl! Keep going! Restrict yourself! Reduce that crime! It can be hard to get out from a system that has run for centuries. Resistance can be drawn back in, reframed and repackaged, so nothing changes.

The key to challenging this kind of misrepresentation is in understanding that our choices, our actions, and even our desires are not free-floating: they spring from our material bodies located in concrete settings which are structured in ways as to open up some possibilities to us while closing down others. Our agency is *situated* in this way, both free and constrained.[11] As such, we can recognise the continuum of sexual violence as a restricting context for women, without denying women's autonomy and our acts of resistance and resilience. With this in mind, understanding how freedom and safety are lived together speaks back to those who argue that focusing on the restrictions around women is adopting a 'victim feminism' – painting women as without agency, done to, never doing. Part of the problem with the charge of victim feminism is that it equates being scared or hurt with being weak, something that can then create resistance in women to speak about their safety work. This can be seen in how Taryn told me, as Theodora did in Chapter One, that she had always felt safe by herself in public.

> Well I've always felt safe walking around by myself at night, during the day, whenever. But there was always this thing where I felt that if I didn't feel safe, that was just me being a coward.

Once the framing changed from one of safety and risk to one of freedom and ease, Taryn was able to tell a different story. One that wasn't as caught in the need to be the strong empowered woman. One that could include the restrictions she made to herself without dismissing these as a failing.

> I don't feel comfortable on the streets. I don't feel comfortable when I walk past groups of men, actually I've walked on the other side of the street to avoid them. If I walk into a carriage and there's a man over there and a seat over there, I'll sit over there. I'll always sit next to a woman. In fact, when I'm with my husband, if there's a man and two seats he'll always sit there. So he does it too. He doesn't want me to sit next to men. I've crossed the street too. And the main thing I think is that I look down, I don't look at them.

Paying attention to how women's actions are caught on a tightrope between safety and freedom can also help to challenge a culture that reprimands women for not taking 'common sense precautions' to protect themselves. What is safe changes based on experience, and we know that experiences are not all the same. Just as Carolyn in Chapter Four learnt to avoid harassment by walking through the park not on the main road, many women may appear to not be using 'common sense', when in fact what they are doing is making a carefully calculated decision. A balancing act born of experience, reinforced throughout our lives. And yet by acting in the way we have been told to, we're made to feel we've done something wrong. Like Meg and Louise below, again we dismiss our knowledge, believing we're probably paranoid, over-reacting.

> I'm really paranoid though, like with everything. With the tube, I usually get off the bus just there and there's a little street here that takes me to my house, and it's like a nice little block so it's not like you hear loads of stories that someone was you know mugged or something, but if I'm walking down there that's

when I won't have my headphones in so I can hear footsteps, even if it's a girl I want to be able to hear footsteps. But I think if there's like one person behind you, even if they aren't following, you always sort of think, oh man, let's keep an eye out on this one. You're just wary everywhere you go. – Meg

I think it might be slightly paranoid behaviour in that we're doing it in situations where we might not necessarily be in danger but I think there is good reason for it. Like I used to live close to a park and there were two rapes in that park a couple of weeks before I moved. One of them was in the middle of the night and the other was at a normal time, like 6 or 7, so these things do happen in fairly open normal public spaces. When you hear this type of thing you think that you're not wrong in carrying out these small adaptations of behaviour. – Louise

These small adaptations go so unnoticed that prevention campaigns can give women safety tips without acknowledging how much they already do, and we can say we do what we want without being aware of the extent of our work. This was seen in the most unexpected finding of the research underpinning this book: that for almost all of the women who used the notebook, they found significantly less *happening* than they initially thought, and yet were *doing* substantially more. Alice talked about the first part back in Chapter One, how being harassed "was a feeling that didn't actually manifest as much as I thought it would". She also told me that she didn't change herself much as she didn't want harassment to restrict what she did.

It's never really made me augment the way I live. I mean I still walk home and I'll still not get a taxi and catch a bus home if it's dark because I object to the idea that I should have to augment my entire experience of life because there are guys who are sick out there and sad.

On reflection, however, Alice found not only that she wasn't being targeted for harassment in the way that she felt like she was, but also that to avoid it she was doing considerably more than she'd thought. Thinking about how she *was* in public, she saw the small changes she was making as about that external awareness mentioned in Chapter Four, a wariness, watching men.

> I do augment my everyday life with those things in mind. I always check men and I watch their behaviour. If I'm on the bus or whatever. It doesn't happen so much in the daytime, though my minor assault happened in the day so now I'm quite suspicious in the daytime anyway because I realise if it can happen in a fucking takeaway at one in the afternoon on a Sunday in bright daylight and that was just completely, nothing of what you expect I guess, what you expect it's going to be. But yeah the things that I do, if I think about my experience of the day, I'm wary of most men. Really, until proven otherwise, if I'm really honest.

These limitations to freedom are not just about actions, limiting our ability to do something, but as seen in the descriptions across this chapter, they are disrupting women's ability to *be*. Safe but not comfortable. Safe but not free. The problem is that our habits hide what we are doing from ourselves and from others, making it easier for us to be blamed when, despite our work, something happens. As shown in the reflections of Taryn and Alice, the shift to considering safety only in connection to freedom helps to undo this, working to increase the stories that can be told both to others and to ourselves. Instead of being limited by being either complimentary – and thus trivial so must be discounted – or threatening – and thus criminal so must be reported – focusing on freedom changes what counts as sexual harassment, as well as why it matters. In this way it helps to move the conversation on from a focus that hides women's work, focusing only on our failures, to one that identifies and names the range and extent of women's ordinary resistance.

SIX

Ordinary resistance

Public space as space for action

Exploring the right amount of panic has revealed the ways in which women are significantly, habitually, restricting their activities, limiting their freedom, in exchange for a sense of safety. We have looked at the evidence that women may be more scared of crime in public space than men, but challenged the idea that this fear is unjustified. Instead it's been shown that gender roles mean we may not be getting the whole story of men's fear, that crime statistics may mean we're not getting the whole story of women's victimisation, and that the shadow of sexual assault may mean we're not measuring the same things anyway. It's also been suggested that the ways in which women's fear of crime alters our behaviour may actually form part of the reason that we experience less crime than men, or at least the types of crime commonly counted in crime surveys. This kind of change is what is meant by 'safety work'.

To try to understand more about how and why we learn to do it, Chapter Three looked at the ways in which the message of 'stranger danger' is particularly gendered and at the meanings which underpin it; mainly that women are responsible for preventing sexual violence at the same time as lacking the common sense needed to do just that. It found that these messages are embedded for many in experiences of intrusive, harassing and abusive men in childhood and adolescence, as well as through the ways that such experiences are responded to by others. Women are taught that we are the thing that causes – and so the thing that can stop – sexual violence, at the same time as being taught to doubt ourselves. The lessons about women's responsibility for preventing sexual violence mixes with gender stereotypes about how to be a blameless woman: polite, compliant, silent. When many young women do speak up, they are treated as though they are mistaken, lying or accountable. Faced with such limitations, the only course of action is to change ourselves.

Chapter Four looked in detail at what these changes are. It addressed the ways in which women's safety work is invisible, and why sometimes we might want it to stay that way, as well as the importance of acknowledging and speaking about it to challenge the ways women are blamed for being sexually assaulted. When this work is recognised we can see it across even the smallest choices and find the messages we've taken from it are buried deep in how we've learnt to be. Not only doubting ourselves, and believing it's our fault, we learn to be quieter, smaller, less visible, less public. From this position we're tasked with trying to determine the right amount of panic.

Chapter Five unpicked this process, starting with the ways in which the adoption of habits can be understood as a learning of embodied principles. Lessons on sexual violence, how to manage and avoid it, are captured by the body, making it hard to see our safety work even when we try. Once absorbed into our habits, the experiences that taught us how to act can be forgotten, often reconfigured as just a choice or common sense. We saw the ways women draw on these habits stored in the body, responding to the environment and unknown men using an escalation calculation to evaluate the safest course of action. That this action is mostly pre-emptive leads us to the catch-22 that lies at the heart of what women are expected to do. What is revealed by examining the reasoning of safety work is that women are caught: blamed if they do not act to prevent sexual violence, but if they act and prevent it they are paranoid. There is no *right* amount of panic; the only times we can measure are the times we get it wrong. With no way to know when we're getting it right, we give up our freedom and are blamed regardless. Like a trap, we're stuck. So how do we get out?

In the quote that opened this book, the American poet Sylvia Plath talks about how she feels her 'whole circle of action' is circumscribed by the fact she is a woman. Femininity is experienced as a boundary, restricting the experiences she can have and the actions she can take. Though the work of many has meant that women's situation has changed since the mid-20th century when Plath was writing, the accounts given across the previous chapters show how much this feeling still resonates. It is so relevant, in fact, that a close comparison can be made to a concept used in research on violence against women: that of 'space for action'. Space for action builds on Norwegian sociologist Eva Lundgren's work on 'life space', used to capture how the motivations of men who are violent towards their partners are, in part, based on a desire to set limits on women's ability to exercise their freedom.[1] The life space of women is decreased as a way of increasing the life space of the men who were violent towards them. This has subsequently been developed into the idea of space for action by researchers at the Child and Woman Abuse Studies Unit in London, and has been used in relation to young people's understandings of rape, trafficking for sexual exploitation, the sexualisation of popular culture, and young women's experiences of sexual agency.[2]

Like the discussion in Chapter Five on the differences between agency and freedom, space for action helps to make clearer the ways in which agency is about acting within the space that is set and freedom is about being able to set the limits of that space itself. This means it is not enough to focus on our actions alone to find a way out: we need to consider the context within which these actions occur and are given meaning. Nicola Gavey, a psychology professor at the University of Auckland, refers to this as the need to focus on 'the cultural conditions of possibility rather than the individual'.[3] The concept of space for action helps us do this, enabling an acknowledgement that our actions are located in particular contexts that reward certain acts and punish others – both explicitly and implicitly – without denying that action is possible. Instead of the problem being located at an individual level, we are able to look at social structures and how these set limits on what avenues for action are available. And instead of the solution being one of individual change, we look instead at how to communicate the collective, something that coincidentally started to happen on a worldwide scale during the writing of this book.

In early October, 2017, an investigation by the *New York Times* revealed decades of sexual assault allegations against the well-known Hollywood film producer Harvey Weinstein.[4] By mid-October, over 50 women had accused him of a range of forms of sexual violence, including flashing, sexual assault and rape.[5] The revelations sparked the use of the hashtag #metoo, encouraging women to share their experiences of sexual harassment. Though the hashtag went viral in the wake of the allegations against Weinstein, the Me Too movement originated in the work of civil rights activist Tarana Burke over a decade earlier.[6] Having experienced sexual assault herself, Burke saw the importance of breaking the sense of isolation and individuation that many survivors feel. As a black woman, Burke particularly felt the need in the communities she worked in, where women and girls of colour have to struggle to find representations that validate their realities. While the allegations of rape and sexual assault against Weinstein were still growing, the popularity of #metoo meant that women began to speak – and be heard – about experiences of sexual harassment across other sectors from Latina farm workers in the United States, represented by the Alianza Nacional de Campesinas, to female ministers in Westminster.[7]

Partly in response to the letter of solidarity sent from the Alianza Nacional de Campesinas to the women of Hollywood, the *Times Up* campaign was launched in the US at the beginning of 2018.[8] The launch included the announcement of a US$13 million legal defence fund to support lower-income women seeking justice for sexual harassment in the workplace, with much of the funding donated by some of the most well-known women working in the American entertainment industry. It also involved eight activists working in and around the issues accompanying eight Hollywood actors to the Golden Globes, to help amplify their activism. These activists included Tarana Burke and Marai Larasi, the director of UK organisation Imkaan which, as mentioned in Chapter Four, has led the work in the UK on the issue of racialised public sexual harassment. Given the popularity and platform brought to the movement through the support of some of the world's most famous women, Burke has said she is fearful that the voices of the communities that Me Too originated in could be lost. This is an important point, and one that speaks to the need for space for action to be understood as an interconnected rather than individual project.

> You know sexual violence knows no race or color or gender or class. But the response to sexual violence does. And so what we're looking at right now is a response to sexual violence. And in these moments, the most marginalized voices always get overshadowed. And that's who I represent in every space I go into, in every room I bring those voices with me. My work will never lose focus on the least of these, on the queer folks, on disabled folks, people with disabilities, what happens when you're a little black girl, a little brown girl. That is who I champion and I will always.[9]

This connects to what was discussed in Chapter Two about the ways that thinking about 'women's' fear of crime can work to hide differences *between* women. These differences, as Burke says here, are not only or even mainly found in our fears and experiences, but more so in the response we receive and what this says about how much we matter. This moment in the movement for women's liberation that Tarana Burke has created means there is a responsibility going forward to ensure the voices she brings with her are those that are brought forward. Doing this is about recognising that increasing our individual space for action is only possible through increasing the circle of action that circumscribes women *as a whole*. Instead of focusing on increasing her own space – or only the spaces she shares – what Burke has crafted in the Me Too movement is a way of increasing the cultural conditions of possibility. What has been made possible is a culture where, instead of being seen in a competition or hierarchy, women's experiences are shared in solidarity. Where instead of being doubted and denied, they are corroborated. They are not collapsed into a singular experience – each 'me too' is different – but together they give the legitimacy that individual experiences struggle to receive. In challenging this individuation, the Me Too movement has shown what happens when there is validation for the meanings we give experience. When we are heard, we speak.

Though the weight of experience may direct our actions in particular ways, if moments like these are seized they can be powerful enough to shift the ways we've been taught to be. Merleau-Ponty, the philosopher who wrote a lot about habit, has a suitably poetic way of describing this; the way our past directs but does not determine us.

> I have made it my abode, that this past, though not a fate, has at least a specific weight and is not a set of events over there, at a distance from me, but the atmosphere of my present. The rationalist's dilemma: either the free act is possible, or it is not – either the event originates in me or is imposed on me from outside, does not apply to our relations with the world and with our past. Our freedom does not destroy our situation, but gears itself to it: as long as we are alive, our situation is open.[10]

If our situation is open, there is a way out and, after thinking through the accounts given across the previous chapters, three interconnected routes become clear. The first is in challenging the ways we think of sexual violence as an individual event, finding validation instead through its commonality. The second is in reframing what we mean when we say resistance, putting women's success at the forefront of the public conversation on sexual violence. And the final path is in reclaiming feminist self-defence from a way of responding to discrete events to a method of unlearning habits held in the body. The final sections will explore these three possibilities in detail, beginning with the one that Tarana Burke's work so powerfully reveals: that sexual violence is not an individual problem.

It's not you – it's him

As research on sexual violence prevention starts to grow, the importance of challenging gender norms becomes clear. The beliefs underpinning all forms of sexual violence, such as men's entitlement and women's passivity, are sustained through gender norms that function on what Patricia Hill Collins has called 'the construct of dichotomous oppositional difference'.[11] This means that what it is to be a woman is understood only in relation to its difference from being a man and vice versa. In a gender order where men are afforded more value than women, the characteristics that are seen to apply to women will therefore always be the opposite of the characteristics we value: if he is strong, she must be weak; if he is big, she must be small; if he is rational, she must be emotional. This creates the gender norms looked at in Chapter Two – expectations of specific attributes, characteristics, or roles allotted to individuals because of their gender. These norms, set up in opposition to each other, are highly successful in reproducing themselves and appearing natural. As the discussion of the concept of intersectionality made clear, they are also affected by the other ways we are positioned in society, such as through our race and class. What the research on how to prevent violence against women and girls reveals is that what is socially expected of us is a stronger driver of our actions than our individual attitudes or the law.[12] As such, work that aims to transform gender roles and stereotypes – for example by offering different models of how to *be* a woman or a man – is better at reducing violence than that which addresses individual attitudes and behaviours in isolation, like those police rape prevention campaigns from Chapter Three.[13]

Talking about the influence of social expectations and gender norms is not the same as saying that sexual violence is necessarily 'expected' of men, but rather that what *is* required of men – that they are sexual initiators, dominant, disconnected – supports the decision of some men to use violence. Though maybe not expected, it is nevertheless unsurprising. And it is not just men who are influenced in this way. Sara reflects on this in thinking about how sexual harassment is sustained by gender norms that teach girls to understand themselves as something to be looked at.

> I haven't really thought about it but I think what it does is perpetuate the inequality between men and women. It perpetuates the 'you're such a clever boy, you're a big strong boy' and 'you're a pretty little girl', pretty and little. And I think that sort of behaviour

– I mean the men in your life that are direct to you probably build you up and don't do that to you, your dad, your uncle, your brother – but I think saying those particular things to very young girls, it must perpetuate this idea, you're one thing, the object, and they're allowed to look at you.

As seen in Chapter Three, gender norms not only teach women to expect men's intrusion, they also restrict the ways they feel able to respond. This is particularly pronounced in childhood where girls are routinely taught that being a good girl is more important than trusting their own experience of the world. Where dominance and assertion is expected of boys, politeness and diffidence is required of girls. Like Sara, both Becky and Louise reflected on this in relation to sexual harassment, thinking about the lack of education they received when younger that gave any kind of message to the contrary.

I feel like we had the period talk far too late and we had the contraception talk far too late and it was just like for God's sake use a condom, this is really awkward for everybody in the room. But we never really had something teaching us to be assertive or thinking of us as young women, and that would have been so much more beneficial for us. – Becky

I find it so much easier to say no to people now and am gradually learning to be rude in response to what I consider rudeness. For instance, being broached by someone in the streets recently who asked for a number I was able to say no and walk on even though they questioned me three times. It makes you think that maybe that's what should be taught to women, that they should respond in kind to the provocation they're being subjected to, they should respond accordingly. But we don't learn different standards of social response. We just have this one level of politeness. – Louise

Their comments here link back to Viola's in Chapter Three about how girls learn they are weaker and more vulnerable not only through the messages of stranger danger but also through the almost unnoticed ways that their actions are restricted. It is not that girls are naturally less assertive or more polite than boys, but that this is how they are *expected to be*, and these social expectations drive behaviour in a more powerful way than we may even be aware of. It can be hard to know there is a different way to be. Ruth describes this in talking about how she learnt, like Louise, that she didn't have to be polite to men who were bothering her. Finding this out was a revelation.

> I remember when eight or nine years ago I started doing things like going with work colleagues to a club or something like that. And you know what it's like in a club with a drunk guy trying to dance with you or something like that and you're really not interested and they're getting a bit annoying and I'm far too polite and laughing about it when actually it's really annoying me, which I'm sure is a common thing. But I remember it being an absolute revelation that a guy tried it on with a colleague and she just turned her back on him. And I was like, 'Oh my God, you can do that?' That was really quite a new thing for me, I was really surprised. Partly because I was so rarely in that situation, but partly because of this fear of confrontation, that I have to be nice, you know what I mean?

Think back to Chapter Two and how one explanation for the fear of crime paradox is that men and boys find it difficult to admit their fear given the expectation that they are fearless. What we are seeing here is the ways in which the expectation of politeness comes to be naturalised for women, part of what defines a 'good girl', making it difficult to act otherwise. Again this norm needs to be understood intersectionally. For working-class women for example it is often not politeness that is expected but anger or 'mouthiness'. This expectation still acts to police behaviour, as expressions of anger are dismissed as invalid, and function to situate them even further from that 'good girl' worth protecting. What all of this means is that effective prevention messages address and challenge these kinds of gendered norms rather than focusing on changing individual women's actions. Going back to the message we saw in the campaign that started Chapter Three – that the vulnerable friend is the one you leave behind – what would be more useful for rape prevention is the message that women can take up space and be trusted to make our own decisions, alongside messages directed at men that challenge their entitlement and the expectation of their dominance.

Instead of being challenged, however, these norms are sustained by consistent messaging across different spaces, most of which rarely address how interlocking positions of inequality influence how a woman is targeted, the support she receives from bystanders, and the response to her in the aftermath. In the failure of most safety campaigns to recognise the extent to which women's daily behaviour is already changed because of our awareness of men's violence, what is reproduced are gender norms about women's weakness and passivity, about our need for protection and innate vulnerability, of men's inevitable aggression and power. And this is only made worse by many representations of sexual violence in popular entertainment, including my personal favourite *Law & Order* as discussed in Chapter Two. But what if we lived in a world where women's safety work was acknowledged for the highly intuitive adaptation that it is? Where women were taught that these changes don't work all the time not because of a problem in us but because we aren't the ones who are responsible? If the evidence is right and changing gender norms is crucial, then making women visible as capable, powerful and skilful in their everyday negotiations is as important as changing the meanings of masculinity where these are about being fearless, in control, and powerful. This suggests that speaking our safety work might hold the key to rape prevention after all, but not in the ways we thought.

A community of corroboration

In order to use women's safety work to challenge gender norms – to see it for the expert negotiation that it is – we need first to reject the ways we've been encouraged to feel paranoid or inept. As looked at in detail during Chapter Three, part of the process of growing up for girls is being taught to doubt their own sense-making of an encounter. Girls are taught that men's intrusion is unremarkable, an acceptable part of life, and that the cause and the solution is in them despite the fact it might feel otherwise. Imagine if, instead of this, we grew up learning that feeling uncomfortable is enough to mean that what the other person is doing *is* inappropriate. Imagine if we learnt that we don't have to rely on escalation or on the opinions of others to define our own experience. Such work would of course be needed alongside work with men and boys to change the meanings of masculinity, and together these kind of interventions could help to challenge the reproduction of gender norms that locate culpability with women and capability with men.

This is about moving from an individual approach, looking at events as though they are one-offs, 'isolated incidents', towards understanding them as individual manifestations of structural problems. Approaching sexual violence like this highlights the need for prevention campaigns that don't focus on rape as an individual event but that understand it as part of a series that for many women begins with intrusion in childhood. Where the message is not solely about reporting such experiences, but about legitimating them as a wrong done *to* you. This is about reframing their source from being located in the bodies of women and girls, to grounded in the decisions of men and boys, decisions that are encouraged and endorsed by wider social structures.

I've witnessed the radical power of this first hand. The process of conducting the study underpinning this book was a form of validation for myself and for many of the women who took part. This was not only, like the Me Too movement, a validation of the multitude of experiences we'd had, but also of those we hadn't. The research site provided the space to consider the times that nothing *really* happened but we had responded anyway, just in case. Our ordinary experiences were suddenly made legitimate in being part of an academic research project. Once legitimated they became speakable, and not only in the context of the study.

When Cathy first mentioned her experience of being molested on a bus at nine years old back in Chapter Three, she spoke about a feeling of doubt, saying, "I'm almost not even sure if it happened." This was despite the ways, as seen in Chapter Five, it made her change her behaviour on public transport. When I caught up with Cathy after she'd had the notebook, she told me she hadn't actually filled anything in. What she'd decided to do instead was to make public what happened to her as a child.

> A few weeks after we met, I was on the train and this guy got on. He was standing there, looking at me, looking around and this other woman got on and sat next to him. She was patient with him but I was not in a happy mood that day and I saw him looking at me so I just looked back, not like 'don't mess with me' but just very neutral. And he went to the woman, 'You're nice you are. But not her, look at her, she's not nice.' And I just went, 'You know what? I got molested at nine years old, I got on a bus and everyone in this carriage they think it doesn't happen but it happens all the fucking time'. I just went ballistic. He was like, 'Sorry I didn't know' and everyone else looked shocked. I was really upset but I thought I'm not going to move. I'm going to hold my ground. I was so embarrassed but I just thought this has to be done. I've done something right, I've just made it public. It was an exorcism. But it wouldn't have happened if we hadn't had our talk.

Our talk shifted something that Cathy had carried for almost 50 years. The research process validated her story, loosening the silence that had surrounded it. No longer something that was about her, it was now something that happened because of him. A him that is anonymous, repeated. A him that is every man who chooses to intrude. This is some of what was seen in the wake of the Weinstein allegations, and it further reveals the interconnectedness of women's space for action. What is needed is a community of corroboration, where the experiences of women and girls are shared, heard, and validated – not only our experiences of sexual violence and harassment but also the work we all do because of it. We know that while our safety work remains hidden, it stays as something women *are* not something they *do*. The times where it doesn't work then become a problem with us – shameful, unspoken, blamed. What is needed is a way to make it visible, to help us speak back to advice that says we don't do enough. What we need to do is find a way to somehow see our success.

Seeing our success

What has been shown with the Me Too movement, as well as through online 'counter-publics' such as *Everyday Sexism* and *Hollaback!,* is the range and extent of the routine harassment women and girls experience across all aspects of their lives.[14] The pre-emptive quality of most safety work, however, means that just the possibility of harassment is often enough for women to limit ourselves. While the work we do remains hidden it is easier to judge others and ourselves, only aware of what we do not do, never talking about what we did. The invisibility of our safety work, of that constant negotiation of the right amount of panic, has meant that women's successful resistance can be discounted, even as we do it. Think for example about the reasons commonly given for the decline in sexual harassment as women age. Taught to locate the cause of men's intrusive practices in our appearance – something about us – women often believe this generational change has to do with the aging body – no longer seen as 'in our prime', we are no longer treated as sexually desirable by unknown men. As seen in Chapter Five, for some women there may be pleasure in this increasing invisibility, for some there may be an unanticipated feeling of loss, but what is so rarely talked about is that the reasons for this decline may not only lie in a change in how our body is perceived but in the success of our work. What if, as women age, *they* limit the intrusion they experience through the strategies they've embodied; that young women experience more because they have yet to develop a range of strategies that might sometimes be working, though we can never know it? As Elizabeth Stanko points out, the fact 'that women's safety work is not, cannot, be successful every time is more a comment on men's violence than on women's failures'.[15] And yet because women are rarely acknowledged as having any awareness about safety or danger, we rarely consider the possibility that we may be getting it right.

Seeing our success, like expanding our space for action, is an interconnected undertaking not an individual task. It involves the recognition that validating ourselves is only possible through validating and supporting the decisions of other women. The process of change begins in an awareness of our actions. From here we can practise conscious intervention on any bodily habits we want to adjust. In effect, we need to know where we are to know where we can be. The revolutionary possibilities in even this small step was revealed by Sophie when we met up after she completed her notebook. It was Sophie who said in Chapter Two she'd been living in jeans and jumpers for six years to avoid harassment, who in Chapter Four would get almost to the tube and "bottle it", feeling too visible and unprotected if not in the clothes she used for safety. When we spoke again, something had changed. Like Alice and Abbey in Chapter One, she found that after she'd been taking note of what happened, though she often felt visible and exposed this wasn't always connected to the present. Over the month she'd been recording experiences of harassment, it had happened once or twice, much less than she'd thought. She told me she'd come to "the realisation that actually people aren't looking at me I'm looking at them".

> Realising that has been really liberating it's like, right, I'm going to wear that top that I want to wear. And it's not like it's been a massive change, you can see I'm still in my black and baggy jeans combo, but at home outside of London I've definitely been rocking out some outfits that I've had and never worn. I bought this amazing dress when I was in Ghana. It's bright blue, tie-dyed, halterneck and it's just so cool and I would never wear it and now I wear it and I feel great in it, and there's other outfits too. I just feel

ownership of my body and I feel a bit more at peace with it all having done this.

Sophie's words here are reminiscent of Jan talking in Chapter Four about how there was no space for women to be at home in their bodies. The ownership Sophie found in herself only came through a process of conscious awareness, and a decision to intervene on habits she'd built up over time. Her experience shows the ways that seeing our work can help to challenge a feeling of unbelonging, through this encouraging a different way of being, at home and at peace in ourselves. As shown in Chapter Five, seeing our work is not endorsing the role women are made to take to attempt to prevent violence against us. Nor is it about blaming women – again – for the ways that we've learnt to adapt. It is about providing room for reflection on the space between restriction and action, and through that finding an invitation to notice how we've been taught to become in the world.

This kind of process, in the words of Simone de Beauvoir, is about uncovering 'how woman is taught to assume her condition, how she experiences this, what universe she finds herself enclosed in, and what escape mechanisms are permitted her'.[16] Once revealed, the ways in which we embody habits can be used to our advantage: to learn and embed a different form of bodily know-how of women's bodies as strong and capable. Mia talks about how a work colleague took this possibility to heart, testing out a different way of being in public space, again with a sense of ownership.

> She decided one day to walk down the street as if she owned it, as if she literally owned the street, and I don't know what changed about her, she didn't necessarily describe about what changed about her body language and about what she said or what she did, but it's a nice exercise because it's easy to start shuffling or walk with your head down.

In revealing the right amount of panic, we're left with this task; where our experiences with individuals and the structures of society have taught us to feel uncertain, seeing our success means we stop dismissing ourselves as stupid, saying that we're probably paranoid, negating how we felt. It is about recognising, as Katie-Lou does, that although we may know that women shouldn't have to change our behaviour, personally, daily, many of us do.

> I do adapt and I don't like it because you should be able to walk down the street naked and do what you want. I completely believe all that. But at the same time that's not what we're brought up to believe, is it? We're brought up to believe that women are careless and then bad stuff happens to them.

We need to practise a different kind of learning, taking notice of the work we're doing and why. If our behaviour comes from years of believing that we can never get it right, we must find a way to start seeing our work for what it is: a reasonable, skilful, strategic response to the messages we've had across our lives. Recognising the sheer scale of women's efforts to avoid, minimise, or cope with men's intrusive practices could help us to change a culture that makes victims responsible for not preventing assault. Finding a space to make our safety work visible, to speak about its origins and its variations, could put an end to campaigns that give women advice on how to keep safe by not being free. We continue to talk about the problem as though women need to take more responsibility for preventing sexual violence. But preventing sexual violence is something women do daily, often without realising it. What is needed is a way to develop awareness of the work of being a woman. And there's one intervention that does just this – feminist self-defence.

Feminist self-defence: learning to unlearn

Across contexts from Kenya to Canada, there is a growing dialogue seeking to reclaim feminist self-defence.[17] Though considered a radical intervention in the 1970s and incorporated into the services offered by many Rape Crisis Centres, critiques of self-defence led to ambivalence about its usefulness and its eventual replacement with prevention initiatives focused largely on giving information about what does and doesn't constitute sexual consent.[18] Luckily, in the past decade there has been a resurgence in considering its potential contribution to sexual violence prevention, a contribution that is based around the way it changes gender norms.

In Aotearoa New Zealand a national network of accredited teachers of feminist self-defence has been in operation for over 30 years. Though originally targeting adult women, the Women's Self Defence Network Wāhine Toa (WSDN-WT) now focuses on school aged girls, delivering their training to almost 10,000 girls each year, as well as delivering to women in communities that are specifically targeted for sexual violence due to geographic, cultural and/or disability-related isolation. In 2016, the outcomes of this work was evaluated using the accounts of over 3,000 participants, from seven-year-old girls to adult aged women, including a high proportion who were Māori and Pasifika.[19] The results reveal that, contrary to accusations that it is victim blaming, feminist self-defence may in fact provide a crucial route for undoing how women and girls have been taught to blame ourselves. The evaluation found significant improvements in the importance girls and young women placed on help-seeking for themselves and others in the aftermath of sexual violence – suggesting the programme helps to challenge the ways that women are taught to be silent. For all groups there was an increased understanding that unwanted sexual touching and sexual assault is not okay and not their fault. The action-based way the programme was delivered increased its effectiveness for Māori girls, particularly when delivered in all Māori groups taught by a Māori teacher. And across women and girls of all ages there were self-reported increases in self-esteem and feeling strong, as well as significant improvements in the confidence they had in their ability to use their skills to defend themselves. Many of these changes remained consistent years after the intervention had been delivered, a key marker of success for primary prevention.

This promising evaluation is not alone. A considerable body of research now exists showing that feminist self-defence has positive consequences for women and girls including increased self-esteem, capability, assertiveness, physical skills and, crucially given the discussion in Chapter Two, a reduction in women's fear of crime.[20] Studies on effective rape prevention have also shown that feminist self-defence is positively associated with rape avoidance, brings no increased risk of physical injury, and can form part of a support process in how it helps to reduce the levels of trauma symptoms experienced in the aftermath of an assault.[21]

Yet in spite of the weight of research in its favour, feminist self-defence is still misunderstood and misrepresented. Mention it today in relation to the prevention of sexual violence and you will usually be met by the questions and criticisms that seem to follow it regardless of evidence of its success. These largely revolve around the claims that self-defence only focuses on stranger attacks, it excludes women with physical limitations, and it upholds an individual rather than a structural approach to violence prevention through its focus on training individual women. There are also the longstanding arguments that prevention should be about changing men's behaviour, not women's, and that ultimately self-defence is victim blaming. However, the fact that this is one of the only forms of violence prevention focused solely on building skills in women and girls means we owe it to ourselves to reconsider its potential.

The first three criticisms sit together and are based in the misunderstanding that feminist self-defence is all about an individual physical response to an individual immediate event, typically a sudden attack by a stranger often in public space. This belief is based on a model of resistance that is focused on the physical, and a model of sexual violence that, as we saw in Chapter Two, dominates representations of rape. It is also one which is commonly associated with martial arts or 'padded attacker' based approaches, both of which have been found to be have more limited effectiveness than a feminist model.[22] Just as feminist research has worked to expand definitions of violence to make visible forms of violence and resistance that sit outside of these models – for example coercive or controlling forms of psychological violence as in the work of Evan Stark, or attitudinal forms of resistance such as those found in the work of Jan Jordan[23] – so too does feminist self-defence come from this more comprehensive understanding.

A review of the literature on women's self-defence found that contrary to the claim that self-defence removes the responsibility from the men who are the cause of the problem and locates the solution – again – with women, feminist self-defence in fact explicitly includes a critical analysis of violence against women which holds perpetrators accountable and challenges victim blame.[24] Through using the concept of sexual violence as a continuum, as discussed in Chapter Three, it draws on an awareness of the interconnectedness of forms of violence, giving validation to those which are missed from reports of crimes against women, and giving space for the types of violence more likely to be perpetrated by men and boys we know. In this way, instead of focusing solely on strategies for addressing one-off events, feminist self-defence helps to resituate sexual violence from being an individual problem to one that both grounds and is grounded by gender inequality. Rather than a false choice between teaching women self-defence or teaching men respect, we start to see the role of feminist self-defence in changing our expectations of gendered behaviour.

What is needed is a rethinking of what we mean when we talk about self-defence; a shift from the idea of it being a response to a discrete event, to a way of defending women against the ways we have been taught to be – doubtful of ourselves and our abilities, alienated from our bodies, self-blaming, scared. This rethinking, however, is hampered by the limitations of language. The very words we have to describe the work directs our attention to the individual not collective – the singular rather than relational or connected 'self', the single act we are defending against or responding to. Recalling the comments made by Dale Spender back in Chapter Three on the process of silencing, some of this has to do with the struggle to communicate women's needs and realities in a language that was not made by or for us. As Spender points out, men for centuries 'have been checking with each other and confirming the accuracy and adequacy of their descriptions and explanations of the world'.[25] Naming, we find, is a collective task, and Audre Lorde may help us here.

For Lorde, '[t]here are no new ideas still waiting in the wings to save us as women, as human. There are only old and forgotten ones, new combinations, extrapolations and recognitions from within ourselves – along with the renewed courage to try them out.'[26] Even when the terms we have to use don't change, then, there is the possibility that new contexts will shift old meanings. Where the meaning of defence moves from being about an individual's actions to a defence against the weight of social norms. Where self-protection becomes not only about protection during a possible event, but a way of building resilience and resistance to the weight of a society which position women as weak, unreliable, and unsafe. Feminist self-defence offers a way of resisting the limitations of gender norms that situate our bodies as something acted on rather than acted *through*. The problem is reoriented from being about the individual, to helping the individual develop a political analysis of why they have been targeted and how men are supported to choose violence. This moves feminist self-defence from a liberal or individual approach to being part of the community of corroboration discussed earlier; a means of forming bonds between and across women that help validate our experiences without collapsing our differences. While physical measures can be learnt and practised, the fundamental skill taught in feminist self-defence is the belief not only in our own capability to respond in situations of immediate threat, but ultimately a belief in women's – all women's – right to be safe *and* free, and a confidence in their abilities to ensure this is respected.[27] It is in this attitudinal work that some of the greatest potential of feminist self-defence lies, particularly in the ways it helps to combat how women and girls are taught to doubt ourselves. As Anna said in Chapter Four, it is about enabling women to feel confident about who they are and how to 'take their space'.

The psychologist Carl Rogers talks about the ability to trust our own meanings and judgements as an outcome of having an internal locus of evaluation.[28] As seen in Chapter Three, when experiences that felt like harassment are reconfigured as at best a compliment or at worse nothing at all, the locus or central point from which we make evaluations shifts from being in ourselves to being in others. We come to make judgements on whether something is or isn't harassment based on whether the man's behaviour escalates for example, or whether other people think that what he did was wrong. The strategies taught by feminist self-defence speak back directly to this, not only in terms of the physical strategies but also in shifting this orientation. It is about resetting the locus of evaluation as being in us; teaching girls and women, as imagined earlier, that feeling uncomfortable is enough to mean that what the other person is doing is inappropriate. It is about teaching skills to help rebuild our trust in women's experiences and abilities – that's *all* women, not only ourselves. In fact, a report for the European Union found that a key component setting feminist self-defence apart from other forms was its ambition 'to offer women and girls opportunities to be in their bodies in confident and connected ways, to experience their self and other women as strong and capable, and to refuse a timid femininity'.[29] And understanding this helps to respond to the charge that it blames the victim.

As discussed in Chapter Five, if keeping ourselves safe is something that is embedded in being a woman, the failure to do so is experienced as there being something wrong *with us*, not just with what we've done. Made responsible for preventing sexual violence at the same time as told we lack the skills to do this, women are unable to prove their capabilities because success, like their work, is invisible. Feminist self-defence can be part of a series of interventions that help to resituate this work from being common sense or natural to being a form of learned behaviour, helping to unearth the lessons behind it hidden deep in the body. As such, it can be understood as not a practice of teaching women what to do, but rather a process of *unlearning* how we've been taught to be.

We can start to see that feminist self-defence doesn't tell women what to do to prevent violence, blaming us for the inevitable times where it fails, but instead it helps to bring to the surface what *we already* do, and invites an exploration of the reasons underpinning it. Through this it challenges rather than creates a culture of victim blame – making safety work visible, speakable and, importantly, *external*. Sexual violence prevention becomes something we do, not something that we are, and the range of skills and techniques taught help to challenge the harmful notion of safety work as common sense. Working to challenge gender norms of women's bodies as acted on rather than as capable, such an approach also gives women the opportunity to practise this different way of being – a chance to feel what it is like to take up space, to speak and be heard, to have their internal sense of a situation be enough to justify action. Feminist self-defence is about repositioning women as capable and rational agents, skilfully and correctly assessing the actions and motivations of others. And this repositioning provides our escape.

Despite what you've been taught, what you experience is not trivial and how you respond is not accidental. We may not be able to ever know the right amount of panic, but together we can begin to take up our right to public space.

The women whose voices fill these pages know the work that we have to do matters. I hope that in reading their testimonies you found some kind of recognition and validation. I hope something they've said about what has happened to them has helped make something that's happened to you make sense. As the poet Adrienne Rich said, 'the connections between and among women are the most feared, the most problematic, and the most potentially transforming force on the planet'.[30] If transformation is possible, but only through connection, then speaking about our safety work may be just the place to start.

Participant list

Abbey, White American, early twenties, heterosexual.
Alice, White British, mid-twenties, queer.
Anna, White British, mid-twenties, heterosexual.
Anne, White British, mid-twenties, straight.
Bea, White British, mid-twenties, heterosexual.
Bec, White Australian, early thirties, lesbian.
Becky, White British, early twenties, bisexual.
Carolyn, White British, mid-twenties, straight.
Cathrin, White German, late twenties, heterosexual.
Cathy, White British, early fifties, heterosexual.
Charlie, White British, late twenties, heterosexual.
Claire, White British, mid-thirties, heterosexual.
Clare, White British, mid-forties, heterosexual.
Delilah, Black African, mid-twenties, bisexual.
Emma, White Australian, early thirties, bisexual.
Gail, White British, early thirties, straight.
Ginger, White Lithuanian, early twenties, straight.
Hannah, White British, mid-twenties, heterosexual.
Jacqueline, White British, early fifties, heterosexual.
Jane, Pakēha New Zealander, late twenties, heterosexual.
Jan, White British, early sixties, heterosexual.
Jeannine, White Canadian, mid-thirties, heterosexual.
Jen, White British, late twenties, heterosexual.
Josina, Black British, late twenties, lesbian.
June, White British, early twenties, straight.
Katie, White British, early twenties, heterosexual.
Katie-Lou, White British, late twenties, heterosexual.
Kirsten, White European, late twenties, bisexual.
Laura, White British, early twenties, heterosexual.
Lisa, White British, early thirties, straight.
Louise, White French, late twenties, heterosexual.

Lucy, White British, early twenties, bisexual.
Luella, White Latvian, late teens, straight.
Mariag, White British, mid-thirties, heterosexual.
Marly, White Swedish, early thirties, lesbian.
Meg, White British, late teens, straight.
Mia, White British, early thirties.
New Mum, Turkish, early thirties, heterosexual.
Nisha, Black Asian, early thirties, heterosexual.
Rosalyn, White British, late twenties, heterosexual.
Rosie, White British, mid-twenties, heterosexual.
Ruth, White British, early forties, heterosexual.
Sara, White British, mid-twenties.
Shelley, British Asian, early thirties, straight.
Sophia, White European, mid-twenties, heterosexual.
Sophie, British Asian, late twenties, straight.
Taryn, White Australian, late thirties, queer.
Theodora, White British, mid-twenties, heterosexual.
Tracey, White British, mid-forties.
Viola, White German, early thirties, heterosexual.

Notes

1   Plath, S. (2000) *The Unabridged Journals of Sylvia Plath*, edited by Karen V. Kukil, New York: Anchor, p 77.

Chapter One: Introduction

1   Gardner, C.B. (1995) *Passing By: Gender and Public Harassment*, Berkeley: University of California Press.

2   Crawford, A., Jones, T., Woodhouse, T. and Young, J. (1990) *The Second Islington Crime Survey*, Middlesex: Centre for Criminology, Middlesex Polytechnic.

3   In May 2016 ActionAid surveyed 2,500 women aged 16 and over through a YouGov poll conducted in major cities across Brazil, India, and Thailand, as well as in the UK. For more information including other findings from their Safe Cities for Women project, visit www.actionaid.org.uk.

4   Australian study: Johnson, M. and Bennett, E. (2015) *Everyday Sexism: Australian Women's Experiences of Street Harassment*, Melbourne: The Australia Institute. Afghanistan study: WCLRF (2015) *Research on Sexual Harassment Against Women in Public Places, Workplace and Educational Institutions of Afghanistan*, Kabul: Women and Children Legal Research Foundation. Canadian study: Lenton, R., Smith, M.D., Fox, J. and Morra, N. (1999) 'Sexual harassment in public places: Experiences of Canadian women', *Canadian Review of Sociology/Revue canadienne de sociologie*, 36(4), pp 517–40. Egyptian study: Hassan, R., Shoukry, A. and Komsan, N.A. (2008) *Clouds in Egypt's Sky: Sexual Harassment from Verbal Harassment to Rape*, Cairo: Egyptian Center for Women's Rights (ECWR).

5   FRA (2014) *Violence Against Women: An EU-Wide Survey Main Results*, European Union Agency for Fundamental Rights, www.fra.europa.eu.

6   For more information about the problems comparing studies in this area see Vera-Gray, F. (2016a) 'Men's stranger intrusions: rethinking street harassment', *Women's Studies International Forum*, 58, pp 9–17.

7   For an excellent overview of the history of activism against street harassment, including the establishment of both the *Hollaback!* and *Stop Street Harassment* websites, see Kearl, H. (2010) *Stop Street Harassment: Making Public Places Safe and Welcoming for Women*, Santa Barbara: Praeger.

8   To see the map, visit the project website: www.harassmap.org

9   Bates, L. (2014) *Everyday Sexism: The Project that Inspired a Worldwide Movement*, London: Simon and Schuster.

[10] For more on the Girls at Dhabas movement, see www.girlsatdhabas.tumblr. com

[11] Phadke, S., Khan, S. and Ranade, S. (2011) *Why Loiter?: Women and Risk on Mumbai Streets*, New Delhi: Penguin Books India.

[12] For an interesting interview with one of the activists behind the march, Winnet Shamuyarira, see Msonza, N. (2014) 'Reflections on the Zimbabwe Mini Skirt March', *Her Zimbabwe*, 23 December, www.herzimbabwe. co.zw/2014/12/reflections-on-the-zimbabwe-miniskirt-march

[13] See the project website: www.stoptellingwomentosmile.com

[14] For detailed information about the methodology of the original study, as well as a more academic treatment of some of the concepts covered in this book, see Vera-Gray, F. (2017a) *Men's Intrusion, Women's Embodiment: A Critical Analysis of Street Harassment*, Oxford: Routledge.

[15] Warr, M. (1985) 'Fear of rape among urban women', *Social Problems*, 32(3), pp 238–50.

[16] The End Violence Against Women Coalition (EVAW) conducted a YouGov poll in early 2016 as part of its campaigning in the London Mayoral elections, including specific questions on safety work. For full poll results see Dahlgreen, W. (2016) 'A third of British women have been groped in public', YouGov, 8 March, www.yougov.co.uk/news/2016/03/08/third-women-groped-public

[17] Chubin, F. (2014) 'You may smother my voice, but you will hear my silence: An autoethnography on street sexual harassment, the discourse of shame and women's resistance in Iran', *Sexualities*, 17(1–2), pp 176–93.

[18] Kelly, L. (2017) 'Foreword', in Vera-Gray (2017a), p xi.

[19] Vera-Gray (2017a).

Chapter Two: Women, fear and crime

[1] For an overview of this literature, see Hale, C. (1996) 'Fear of Crime: A Review of the Literature', *International Review of Victimology*, 4(2), pp 79–150.

[2] Elizabeth Stanko has written extensively on a feminist critique of the fear of crime paradox. See for example: Stanko, E.A. (1993b) 'The case of fearful women: Gender, personal safety and fear of crime', *Women and Criminal Justice*, 4(1), pp 117–135; Stanko, E.A. (1993a) 'Ordinary Fear: Women, Violence, and Personal Safety', in P.B. Bart and E.G. Moran (eds) *Violence Against Women: The Bloody Footprints*, Newbury Park: Sage, pp 155–64; Stanko, E.A. (1995) 'Women, crime, and fear', *The Annals of the American Academy of Political and Social Science*, 539(1), pp 46–58.

[3] Brown, J. (2011) 'We mind and we care but have things changed? Assessment of progress in the reporting, investigating and prosecution of allegations of rape', *Journal of Sexual Aggression*, 17(3), pp 263–72. Also for an analysis of rape reporting across European Union member states, see: Regan, L. and Kelly, L. (2003) *'Rape: Still a forgotten issue'. Briefing Document for*

Strengthening the Linkages: Consolidating the European Network Project, London: Child and Woman Abuse Studies Unit, London Metropolitan University.

4   Liska, A.E., Sanchirico, A. and Reed, M.D. (1988) 'Fear of crime and constrained behavior specifying and estimating a reciprocal effects model', *Social Forces*, 66(3), pp 827–37.

5   Feminist linguistics Professor Deborah Cameron has cleverly debunked the appearance that women speak more than men as a myth, both in her highly readable book, Cameron, D. (2007) *The Myth of Mars and Venus*, Oxford: Oxford University Press, and online through her blog, www.debuk.wordpress.com

6   Collins, P.H. (1986) 'Learning from the Outsider Within: The Sociological Significance of Black Feminist Thought', *Social Problems*, 33(6), pp S14–S32.

7   Crenshaw, K. (1991) 'Race, gender, and sexual harassment', *Southern Californian Law Review*, 65, pp 1467–76.

8   For studies focused on men's fear of crime and the impact of gender socialisation, see: Goodey, J. (1997) 'Boys don't cry: Masculinities, fear of crime and fearlessness', *The British Journal of Criminology*, 37(3), pp 401–18; Day, K., Stump, C. and Carreon, D. (2003) 'Confrontation and loss of control: Masculinity and men's fear in public space', *Journal of Environmental Psychology*, 23(3), pp 311–22; Sutton, R.M. and Farrall, S. (2004) 'Gender, socially desirable responding and the fear of crime: Are women really more anxious about crime?', *British Journal of Criminology*, 45(2), pp 212–24.

9   This term is used by Esther Madriz in Madriz, E. (1997a) *Nothing Bad Happens to Good Girls: Fear of Crime in Women's Lives*, Berkeley: University of California Press, drawing from the work of Stuart Hall and colleagues in Hall, S., Critcher, C., Jefferson, T., Clarke, J. and Roberts, B. (1978) *Policing the Crisis: Mugging, Law and Order, and the State,* London: MacMillan Press.

10   Britto, S., Hughes, T., Saltzman, K. and Stroh, C. (2007) 'Does 'special' mean young, white and female? Deconstructing the meaning of 'special' in Law and Order: Special Victims Unit', *Journal of Criminal Justice and Popular Culture*, 14(1), pp 39–57.

11   Madriz, E. (1997b) 'Images of criminals and victims: A study on women's fear and social control', *Gender and Society*, 11(3), pp 342–56.

12   Useful discussions of the intersections of gender and race in women's fear of crime include: Day, K. (1999) 'Embassies and sanctuaries: women's experiences of race and fear in public space', *Environment and Planning D: Society and Space*, 17(3), pp 307–28; Madriz (1997a); and Pain, R. (2001) 'Gender, race, age and fear in the city', *Urban Studies*, 38(5–6), pp 899–913.

13   For examples of personal safety alarms and apps marketed at women, see www.womenonguard.com and www.boobytrapbras.com

14   Riger, S. and Gordon, M.T. (1981) 'The fear of rape: A study in social control', *Journal of Social Issues*, 37(4), pp 71–92.

15   Ferraro, K.F. (1996) 'Women's fear of victimization: Shadow of sexual assault?', *Social Forces*, 75(2), pp 667–90.

[16] McNeil, S. (1987) 'Flashing: Its effect on women', in Hanmer, J. and Maynard, M. (eds) *Women, Violence and Social Control*, Basingstoke: Macmillan, pp 93–109.

[17] See Ferraro (1996).

[18] Hickman, S. and Muehlenhard, C.L. (1997) 'College women's fears and precautionary behaviors relating to acquaintance rape and stranger rape', *Psychology of Women Quarterly*, 21(4), pp 527–47.

[19] Two studies on victim blaming in relation to rape taken three decades apart show the consistency of blame across time: Burt, M.R. (1980) 'Cultural myths and support for rape', *Journal of Personality and Social Psychology*, 38, pp 217–30; Gavey, N. (2013) *Just Sex?: The Cultural Scaffolding of Rape*, East Sussex: Routledge.

[20] Madriz (1997a).

[21] Home Office, Ministry of Justice and Office for National Statistics (2013) *An Overview of Sexual Offending in England and Wales*, Official Statistics Bulletin, www.gov.uk/government/statistics/an-overview-of-sexual-offending-in-england-and-wales

[22] Office for National Statistics (2016) 'Chapter Four: Intimate personal violence and partner abuse', in *Compendium: Focus on Violent Crime and Sexual Offending Year ending March 2015*, www.ons.gov.uk/peoplepopulationandcommunity/crimeandjustice/compendium/focusonviolentcrimeandsexualoffences/yearendingmarch2015/chapter4intimatepersonalviolenceandpartnerabuse

[23] World Health Organization, Department of Reproductive Health and Research, London School of Hygiene and Tropical Medicine (2013) *Global and Regional Estimates of Violence Against Women: Prevalence and Health Effects of Intimate Partner Violence and Non-Partner Violence*, Italy: World Health Organization.

[24] Smith, M.D. (1988) 'Women's fear of violent crime: An exploratory test of a feminist hypothesis', *Journal of Family Violence*, 3(1), pp 29–38.

Chapter Three: It's all part of growing up

[1] Sanghani, R. (2015) 'Police rape prevention poster 'blames sexual assault victims'', *Telegraph*, 8 April, www.telegraph.co.uk/women/womens-life/11522485/Police-rape-prevention-poster-blames-sexual-assault-victims.html

[2] For the Essex campaign, see Somers, J. (2015) 'Essex Police Defend Student Safety Poster Campaign After Petition Brands It 'Victim Blaming'', Huffington Post UK, 29 September, www.huffingtonpost.co.uk/2015/09/29/essex-police-deny-claims_n_8214272.html. For the West Mercia campaign, see BBC News (2012) 'West Mercia Police apologise over rape campaign poster', 2 August, www.bbc.co.uk/news/uk-england-hereford-worcester-19091566. For the West Yorkshire campaign, you can visit the campaign site: www.westyorkshire.police.uk/party-animals

[3] This particular campaign has been discontinued; however, the image can be seen in this article on rape prevention posters: Wignall, L. (2015)

'Can anti-rape poster campaigns help prevent attacks?', BBC Newsbeat, 8 April, www.bbc.co.uk/newsbeat/article/32219357/can-anti-rape-poster-campaigns-help-prevent-attacks

[4] For information on the #homesafeselfie campaign, see www.tfl.gov.uk/info-for/media/press-releases/2014/september/share-a-homesafeselfie---safer-travel-at-night

[5] Stanko. E. (1990) *Everyday Violence: Women's and Men's Experience of Personal Danger*, London: Pandora Press.

[6] Kelly, L. (2016) 'The Conducive Context of Violence Against Women and Girls', *Discover Society*, 1 March, www.discoversociety.org/2016/03/01/theorising-violence-against-women-and-girls

[7] Goodey, J. (1997) 'Boys don't cry: Masculinities, fear of crime and fearlessness', *The British Journal of Criminology*, 37(3), pp 401–18.

[8] See CEOP (2011) 'Exposed' description and film: www.youtube.com/watch?v=4ovR3FF_6us

[9] For a full description of the problems with the term 'revenge pornography' and the benefits of 'image-based sexual abuse', see McGlynn, C. and Rackley, E. (2017) 'Image-based sexual abuse', *Oxford Journal of Legal Studies*, 37(3), pp 534–61.

[10] See Fine, M. (1988) 'Sexuality, schooling, and adolescent females: The missing discourse of desire', *Harvard Educational Review*, 58(1), pp 29–54. Also Vera-Gray, F. (2017b) 'Girlhood, agency, and embodied space for action', in Formark, B., Mulari, H. and Voipio, M. (eds) *Nordic Girlhoods: New Perspectives and Outlooks,* New York: Palgrave Macmillan, pp 127–35.

[11] Madriz (1997a).

[12] Kelly, L. (1988) *Surviving Sexual Violence*, Oxford: Polity Press.

[13] Spender, D. (1985) *Man Made Language* (2nd edition), New York: Routledge and Kegan Paul, p 59.

Chapter Four: The work of creating safety

[1] For a useful exploration of the concept of invisible work see DeVault, M.L. (2014) 'Mapping invisible work: Conceptual tools for social justice projects', *Sociological Forum*, 29(4), pp 775–90.

[2] Fishman, P. (1978) 'Interaction: The Work Women Do', *Social Problems,* 25, pp 397–406: p 405.

[3] Rollins, J. (1985) *Between Women: Domestics and Their Employers*, Philadelphia: Temple University Press.

[4] Oakley, A. (1974) *The Sociology of Housework,* New York: Pantheon Books.

[5] Hochschild, A.R. (1983) *The Managed Heart: Commercialization of Human Feeling,* Berkeley: University of California Press.

[6] Kelly (2017), p xi.

[7] Lewis, R., Sharp, E., Remnant, J. and Redpath, R. (2015) "Safe spaces': experiences of feminist women-only space', *Sociological Research Online,* 20(4), pp 1–14.

8   See for example Cowan, G. (2000) 'Women's hostility toward women and rape and sexual harassment myths', *Violence against Women*, 6(3), pp 238–46.
9   Riger and Gordon (1981).
10 Schepple, K. and Bart, P. (1983) 'Through Women's Eyes: Defining Danger in the Wake of Sexual Assault', *Journal of Social Issues*, 39(2), pp 63–80.
11 For information on Imkaan, visit www.imkaan.org.uk; for the End Violence Against Women coalition, visit www.evaw.org.uk. Information on their joint work on public sexual harassment is available at www.endviolenceagainstwomen.org.uk/powerful-new-film-black-women-speak-out-about-racist-sexual-harassment
12 To view the films and learn more about the work of Purple Drum, visit https://purpledrum.me
13 For an exploration of this concept in the work of Simone de Beauvoir see Arp, K. (1995) 'Beauvoir's Concept of Bodily Alienation', in Simons, M. (ed) *Feminist Interpretations of Simone de Beauvoir*, Pennsylvania: The Pennsylvania State University Press, pp 161–77.
14 For an interesting exploration of the genealogy of manspreading see Jane, E. (2016) "Dude ... stop the spread': Antagonism, agonism, and #manspreading on social media', *International Journal of Cultural Studies*, 20(5), pp 459–75.

Chapter Five: The right amount of panic

1   Merleau-Ponty, M. (2002) *Phenomenology of Perception*, translated by C. Smith, Oxford: Routledge, p 169.
2   For more on the process of habituation in relation to men's intrusive practices see Vera-Gray (2017a).
3   For a fascinating discussion of the differences between agency and freedom see Miriam, K. (2007) 'Toward a Phenomenology of Sex-Right: Reviving Radical Feminist Theory of Compulsory Heterosexuality', *Hypatia*, 22(1), pp 210–28.
4   Coy, M. (2009a) 'This Body Which is Not Mine: The Notion of the Habit Body, Prostitution and (Dis)Embodiment', *Feminist Theory*, 10(1), pp 61–75.
5   Heller, J. (1999) *Catch-22*, New York: Simon and Schuster, p 532.
6   Wise, S. and Stanley, L. (1987) *Georgie Porgie: Sexual Harassment in Everyday Life*, London: Pandora Press, p 171.
7   Gladman, A. and Heal, A. (2017) *Child Sexual Exploitation After Rotherham*, London: Jessica Kingsley.
8   Jay, A. (2014) *Independent Inquiry into Child Sexual Exploitation in Rotherham: 1997–2013*, Rotherham Metropolitan Borough Council, www.rotherham.gov.uk/download/downloads/id/1407/independent_inquiry_cse_in_rotherham.pdf
9   *The Sunday Times* (2011) 'Revealed: conspiracy of silence on UK sex gangs', 5 January, www.thetimes.co.uk/article/revealed-conspiracy-of-silence-on-uk-sex-gangs-gpg5vqsqz9h

[10] An analysis of media reporting of the case showed that a singular narrative was constructed, drawing on Orientalist discourses on the dangerous, male, Muslim, 'other' as threat to white, female, sexual purity. This narrative structures both what is known about the case as well as how this knowledge was, and still is, deployed by both the media and the state. For more on this see Larasi, M. (2013) '[Re]Constructing the Sexual Terrorist: The Racialisation of Contemporary Media Debates on Child Sexual Exploitation', MA Dissertation, University of Bedfordshire.

[11] Vera-Gray, F. (2016b) 'Situating Agency', *Trouble and Strife*, www. troubleandstrife.org/2016/05/situating-agency/

Chapter Six: Ordinary resistance

[1] Lundgren, E. (1998) 'The Hand that Strikes and Comforts: Gender Construction and the Tension Between Body and Soul', in Dobash, R.E. and Dobash, R.P. (eds) *Rethinking Violence Against Women*, Thousand Oaks, CA: Sage, pp 169–98.

[2] See (in order of topic listed in text): Jeffner, S. (2000) 'Different space for action: The everyday meaning of young people's perception of rape', Presentation at ESS Faculty Seminar, University of North London, May; Kelly, L. (2003) 'The wrong debate: Reflections on why force is not the key issue with respect to trafficking in women for sexual exploitation', *Feminist Review*, 73, pp 139–44; Coy, M. (2009b) 'Milkshakes, lady lumps and growing up to want boobies: how the sexualisation of popular culture limits girls' horizons', *Child Abuse Review*, 18(6), pp 372–83; Vera-Gray (2017b).

[3] Gavey, N. (2012) 'Beyond "empowerment"? Sexuality in a sexist world', *Sex Roles*, 66(11–12), pp 718–24: p 722.

[4] Kantor, J. and Twohey, M. (2017) 'Harvey Weinstein Paid Off Sexual Harassment Accusers for Decades', *New York Times,* 5 October, www. nytimes.com/2017/10/05/us/harvey-weinstein-harassment-allegations. html

[5] Davis, C. and Khomami, N. (2017) 'Harvey Weinstein: a list of the women who have accused him', *Guardian,* 21 October, www.theguardian.com/ film/2017/oct/11/the-allegations-against-harvey-weinstein-what-we-know-so-far

[6] Garcia, S.E. (2017) 'The Woman Who Created #MeToo Long Before Hashtags', *New York Times,* 20 October, www.nytimes.com/2017/10/20/ us/me-too-movement-tarana-burke.html

[7] *Time* (2017) '700,000 Female Farmworkers Say They Stand With Hollywood Actors Against Sexual Assault', 10 November, http://time. com/5018813/farmworkers-solidarity-hollywood-sexual-assault; Castle, S. (2017) 'Sexual Harassment Claims Surface in U.K. Parliament', *New York Times,* 30 October, www.nytimes.com/2017/10/30/world/europe/ sexual-harassment-british-parliament.html

8   For more information on the 'Time's Up' movement, see the project website: www.timesupnow.com

9   Guerra, C. (2017) 'Tarana Burke, the activist behind 'Me Too,' on where movement goes from here', *Boston Globe*, 19 October, www.bostonglobe.com/lifestyle/2017/10/19/tarana-burke-activist-behind-too-where-movement-goes-from-here/YGV7Epp4wMNB9R7Qjcp9RN/story.html

10 Merleau-Ponty (2002), p 514.

11 Collins (1986).

12 Alexander-Scott, M., Bell, E. and Holden, J. (2016) *DFID Guidance Note: Shifting Social Norms to Tackle Violence Against Women and Girls (VAWG)*, London: VAWG Helpdesk, www.gov.uk/government/uploads/system/uploads/attachment_data/file/507845/Shifting-Social-Norms-tackle-Violence-against-Women-Girls3.pdf

13 Heise, L. and Fulu, E. (2014) *What Works to Prevent Violence Against Women and Girls. State of the Field of Violence Against Women and Girls: What do we Know and What are the Knowledge Gaps?*, London: DFID, www.gov.uk/government/uploads/system/uploads/attachment_data/file/337603/What-know-what-knowledge-gaps-D.pdf

14 The concept of online counter-publics was developed by Micheal Salter in relation to sexual violence in Salter, M. (2013) 'Justice and revenge in online counter-publics: Emerging responses to sexual violence in the age of social media', *Crime, Media, Culture*, 9(3), pp 225–42. This was drawn on specifically in relation to online activism and street harassment by Bianca Fileborn in Fileborn, B. (2014) 'Online activism and street harassment: Digital justice or shouting into the ether?', *Griffith Journal of Law and Human Dignity*, 2(1), pp 32–51.

15 Stanko (1990), p 87.

16 de Beauvoir, S. (2011) *The Second Sex*, translated by C. Borde and S. Malovany-Chevallier, London: Vintage, p 289.

17 For Kenyan study, see Sarnquist, C., Omondi, B., Sinclair, J., Gitau, C., Paiva, L., Mulinge, M., Corn, D. and Maldonado, Y. (2014) 'Rape prevention through empowerment of adolescent girls', *Pediatrics*, 133. For Canadian study, see Senn, C.Y., Eliasziw, M., Barata, P. C., Thurston, W.E., Newby-Clark, I.R., Radtke, H.L., and Hobden, K.L. (2015) 'Efficacy of a sexual assault resistance program for university women', *New England Journal of Medicine*, 372(24), pp 2326–35.

18 Kelly, L. and Sharp-Jeffs, N. (2016) *Knowledge and Know-How: The Role of Self-Defence in the Prevention of Violence against Women*, Report prepared for the Directorate General for Internal Policies, Citizen's Rights and Constitutional Affairs: Women's Rights and Gender Equality, European Union, www.europarl.europa.eu/supporting-analyses

19 For full evaluation report see Jordan, J. and Mossman, E. (2016) *Skills for Safety: An Evaluation of the Value, Impact and Outcomes of the Girls' and Women's Self Defence in the Community*, WSDN-WT, http://wsdn.org.nz/research/. For academic articles based on the study, see Jordan, J. and Mossman, E. (2017a) '"Back Off Buddy, This Is My Body, Not Yours":

Empowering Girls Through Self-Defense', *Violence Against Women*, https://doi.org/10.1177/1077801217741217; Jordan, J. and Mossman, E. (2017b) '"Don't Ever Give Up!" Resisting Victimhood Through Self-Defense', *Journal of Interpersonal Violence*, doi: 10.1177/0886260517744760.

[20] For some good overviews of the research on feminist self-defence, see Brecklin, L.R. and Ullman, S.E. (2005) 'Self-defense or assertiveness training and women's responses to sexual attacks', *Journal of Interpersonal Violence*, 20(6), pp 738–62; Brecklin, L.R. (2008) 'Evaluation outcomes of self-defense training for women: A review', *Aggression and Violent Behavior*, 13(1), pp 60–76; Hollander, J.A. (2014) 'Does self-defense training prevent sexual violence against women?', *Violence Against Women*, 20(3), pp 252–269; Hollander, J.A. (2004) '"I Can Take Care of Myself" The Impact of Self-Defense Training on Women's Lives', *Violence Against Women*, 10(3), pp 205–35; Seith, C. and Kelly, L. (2003) *Achievements Against the Grain: Self-Defence Training for Women and Girls in Europe*, Child and Woman Abuse Studies Unit, London Metropolitan University; McDaniel, P. (1993) 'Self-defense training and women's fear of crime', *Women's Studies International Forum*, 16(1), pp 37–45.

[21] Brecklin, L.R. and Ullman, S.E. (2004) 'Correlates of Postassault Self-Defense/Assertiveness Training Participation for Sexual Assault Survivors', *Psychology of Women Quarterly*, 28(2), pp 147–58; Senn, C.Y., Eliasziw, M., Barata, P.C., Thurston, W.E., Newby-Clark, I.R., Radtke, H.L. and Hobden, K.L. (2015) 'Efficacy of a sexual assault resistance program for university women', *The New England Journal of Medicine*, 372, pp 2326–35.

[22] Kelly and Sharp-Jeffs (2016).

[23] See Stark, E. (2009) 'Rethinking Coercive Control', *Violence Against Women*, 15(12), pp 1509–25; Jordan, J. (2005) 'What would MacGyver do? The meaning (s) of resistance and survival', *Violence Against Women*, 11(4), pp 531–59; Jordan, J. (2008) *Serial Survivors: Women's Narratives of Surviving Rape*, Sydney: Federation Press.

[24] See Kelly and Sharp-Jeffs (2016).

[25] Spender (1985), p 4.

[26] Lorde, A. (2007) 'Poetry is Not a Luxury', in Lorde, A. *Sister Outsider: Essays and Speeches by Audre Lorde*, Berkeley, CA: Crossing Press, p 38.

[27] Jordan and Mossman (2016), p 4.

[28] Rogers, C. (1961) *On Becoming a Person: A Therapist's View of Psychotherapy*, London: Constable.

[29] Kelly and Sharp-Jeffs (2016), p 14.

[30] Rich, A. (1979) 'Disloyal to Civilization: Feminism, Racism, Gynophobia', in Rich, A. (ed) *On Lies, Secrets, and Silence*, New York: Norton, pp 275–310.

References

Alexander-Scott, M., Bell, E. and Holden, J. (2016) *DFID Guidance Note: Shifting Social Norms to Tackle Violence Against Women and Girls (VAWG)*, London: VAWG Helpdesk, www.gov.uk/government/uploads/system/uploads/attachment_data/file/507845/Shifting-Social-Norms-tackle-Violence-against-Women-Girls3.pdf

Arp, K. (1995) 'Beauvoir's Concept of Bodily Alienation', in Simons, M. (ed) *Feminist Interpretations of Simone de Beauvoir*, Pennsylvania: The Pennsylvania State University Press, pp 161–77.

Bates, L. (2014) *Everyday Sexism: The Project that Inspired a Worldwide Movement*, London: Simon and Schuster.

BBC News (2012) 'West Mercia Police apologise over rape campaign poster', 2 August, www.bbc.co.uk/news/uk-england-hereford-worcester-19091566

Britto, S., Hughes, T., Saltzman, K. and Stroh, C. (2007) 'Does 'special' mean young, white and female? Deconstructing the meaning of 'special' in Law and Order: Special Victims Unit', *Journal of Criminal Justice and Popular Culture*, 14(1), pp 39–57.

Brown, J. (2011) 'We mind and we care but have things changed? Assessment of progress in the reporting, investigating and prosecution of allegations of rape', *Journal of Sexual Aggression*, 17(3), pp 263–72.

Burt, M.R. (1980) 'Cultural myths and support for rape', *Journal of Personality and Social Psychology*, 38, pp 217–30.

Cameron, D. (2007) *The Myth of Mars and Venus*, Oxford: Oxford University Press,

Castle, S. (2017) 'Sexual Harassment Claims Surface in U.K. Parliament', *New York Times*, 30 October www.nytimes.com/2017/10/30/world/europe/sexual-harassment-british-parliament.html

Chubin, F. (2014) 'You may smother my voice, but you will hear my silence: An autoethnography on street sexual harassment, the discourse of shame and women's resistance in Iran', *Sexualities*, 17(1–2), pp 176–93.

Collins, P.H. (1986). 'Learning from the Outsider Within: The Sociological Significance of Black Feminist Thought', *Social Problems*, 33(6), pp S14–S32.

Cowan, G. (2000) 'Women's hostility toward women and rape and sexual harassment', myths, *Violence Against Women*, 6(3), pp 238–46.

Coy, M. (2009a) 'This Body Which is Not Mine: The Notion of the Habit Body, Prostitution and (Dis)Embodiment', *Feminist Theory*, 10(1), pp 61–75.

Coy, M. (2009b) 'Milkshakes, lady lumps and growing up to want boobies: how the sexualisation of popular culture limits girls' horizons', *Child Abuse Review*, 18(6), pp 372–83.

Crawford, A., Jones, T., Woodhouse, T. and Young, J. (1990) *The Second Islington Crime Survey*, Middlesex: Centre for Criminology, Middlesex Polytechnic.

Crenshaw, K. (1991) 'Race, gender, and sexual harassment', *Southern Californian Law Review*, 65, pp 1467–76.

Dahlgreen, W. (2016) 'A third of British women have been groped in public', YouGov, 8 March, www.yougov.co.uk/news/2016/03/08/third-women-groped-public

Davis, C. and Khomami, N. (2017) 'Harvey Weinstein: a list of the women who have accused him', *Guardian*, 21 October, www.theguardian.com/film/2017/oct/11/the-allegations-against-harvey-weinstein-what-we-know-so-far

Day, K. (1999) 'Embassies and sanctuaries: women's experiences of race and fear in public space', *Environment and Planning D: Society and Space*, 17(3), pp 307–28.

Day, K., Stump, C. and Carreon, D. (2003) 'Confrontation and loss of control: Masculinity and men's fear in public space', *Journal of Environmental Psychology*, 23(3), pp 311–22.

de Beauvoir, S. (2011) *The Second Sex*, translated by C. Borde and S. Malovany-Chevallier, London: Vintage.

DeVault, M.L. (2014) 'Mapping invisible work: Conceptual tools for social justice projects', *Sociological Forum*, 29(4), pp 775–90.

Ferraro, K.F. (1996) 'Women's fear of victimization: Shadow of sexual assault?', *Social Forces*, 75(2), pp 667–90.

Fileborn, B. (2014) 'Online activism and street harassment: Digital justice or shouting into the ether?', *Griffith Journal of Law and Human Dignity*, 2(1), pp 35–51.

Fine, M. (1988) 'Sexuality, schooling, and adolescent females: The missing discourse of desire', *Harvard Educational Review*, 58(1), pp 29–54.

Fishman, P. (1978) 'Interaction: The Work Women Do', *Social Problems*, 25, pp 397–406.

FRA (2014) *Violence Against Women: An EU-Wide Survey Main Results*, European Union Agency for Fundamental Rights, http://fra.europa.eu/sites/default/les/fra-2014-vaw-surveymain-results_en.pdf

Gardner, C.B. (1995) *Passing By: Gender and Public Harassment*, Berkeley: University of California Press.

Garcia, S.E. (2017) 'The Woman Who Created #MeToo Long Before Hashtags', *New York Times*, 20 October, www.nytimes.com/2017/10/20/us/me-too-movement-tarana-burke.html

Gavey, N. (2012) 'Beyond "empowerment"? Sexuality in a sexist world', *Sex Roles*, 66(11–12), pp 718–24.

Gavey, N. (2013) *Just Sex? The Cultural Scaffolding of Rape*, East Sussex: Routledge.

Gladman, A. and Heal, A. (2017) *Child Sexual Exploitation After Rotherham*, London: Jessica Kingsley.

Goodey, J. (1997) 'Boys don't cry: Masculinities, fear of crime and fearlessness', *The British Journal of Criminology*, 37(3), pp 401–18.

Guerra, C. (2017) 'Tarana Burke, the activist behind 'Me Too,' on where movement goes from here', *Boston Globe*, 19 October, www.bostonglobe.com/lifestyle/2017/10/19/tarana-burke-activist-behind-too-where-movement-goes-from-here/YGV7Epp4wMNB9R7Qjcp9RN/story.html

Hale, C. (1996) 'Fear of Crime: A Review of the Literature', *International Review of Victimology*, 4(2), pp 79–150.

Hall, S., Critcher, C., Jefferson, T., Clarke, J. and Roberts, B. (1978) *Policing the Crisis: Mugging, Law and Order, and the State*, London: Macmillan Press.

Heller, J. (1999) *Catch-22*, New York: Simon and Schuster.

Hickman, S. and Muehlenhard, C.L. (1997) 'College women's fears and precautionary behaviors relating to acquaintance rape and stranger rape', *Psychology of Women Quarterly*, 21(4), pp 527–47.

Heise, L. and Fulu, E. (2014) *What Works to Prevent Violence Against Women and Girls. State of the Field of Violence Against Women and Girls: What do we Know and What are the Knowledge Gaps?*, London: DFID, www.gov.uk/government/uploads/system/uploads/attachment_data/file/337603/What-know-what-knowledge-gaps-D.pdf

Hochschild, A.R. (1983) *The Managed Heart: Commercialization of Human Feeling*, Berkeley: University of California Press.

Home Office, Ministry of Justice, and Office of National Statistics (2013) *An Overview of Sexual Offending in England and Wales*, Official Statistics Bulletin, www.gov.uk/government/statistics/an-overview-of-sexual-offending-in-england-and-wales

Jane, E. (2016) "Dude… stop the spread:' Antagonism, agonism, and #manspreading on social media', *International Jounral of Cultural Studies*, 20(5), pp 459–75.

Jay, A. (2014) *Independent Inquiry Into Child Sexual Exploitation in Rotherham: 1997–2013*, Rotherham Metropolitan Borough Council, www.rotherham.gov.uk/download/downloads/id/1407/independent_inquiry_cse_in_rotherham.pdf

Jeffner, S. (2000) 'Different space for action: The everyday meaning of young people's perception of rape', Presentation at ESS Faculty Seminar, University of North London, May.

Johnson, M. and Bennett, E. (2015) *Everyday Sexism: Australian Women's Experiences of Street Harassment*, Melbourne: The Australia Institute.

Jordan, J. (2005) 'What would MacGyver do? The meaning (s) of resistance and survival', *Violence Against Women*, 11(4), pp 531–59.

Jordan, J. (2008) *Serial Survivors: Women's Narratives of Surviving Rape*, Sydney: Federation Press.

Jordan, J. and Mossman, E. (2016) *Skills for Safety: An Evaluation of the Value, Impact and Outcomes of the Girls' and Women's Self Defence in the Community*, WSDN-WT, http://wsdn.org.nz/research/

Jordan, J., and Mossman, E. (2017a) '"Back Off Buddy, This Is My Body, Not Yours": Empowering Girls Through Self-Defense', *Violence Against Women*, https://doi.org/10.1177/1077801217741217

Jordan, J. and Mossman, E. (2017b) '"Don't Ever Give Up!" Resisting Victimhood Through Self-Defense', *Journal of Interpersonal Violence*, doi: 10.1177/0886260517744760

Kantor, J. and Twohey, M. (2017) 'Harvey Weinstein Paid Off Sexual Harassment Accusers for Decades', *New York Times*, 5 October, www.nytimes.com/2017/10/05/us/harvey-weinstein-harassment-allegations.html

Kearl, H. (2010) *Stop Street Harassment: Making Public Places Safe and Welcoming for Women*, Santa Barbara: Praeger.

Kelly, L. (1988) *Surviving Sexual Violence*, Oxford: Polity Press.

Kelly, L. (2003) 'The wrong debate: Reflections on why force is not the key issue with respect to trafficking in women for sexual exploitation', *Feminist Review*, 73, pp 139–44.

Kelly, L. and Sharp-Jeffs, N. (2016) *Knowledge and Know-How: The Role of Self-Defence in the Prevention of Violence against Women*, Report prepared for the Directorate General for Internal Policies, Citizen's Rights and Constitutional Affairs: Women's Rights and Gender Equality, European Union, www.europarl.europa.eu/supporting-analyses

Kelly, L. (2016) 'The Conducive Context of Violence Against Women and Girls', *Discover Society*, 1 March, www.discoversociety.org/2016/03/01/theorising-violence-against-women-and-girls

Larasi, M. (2013) '[Re]Constructing the Sexual Terrorist: The Racialisation of Contemporary Media Debates on Child Sexual Exploitation', MA Dissertation, University of Bedfordshire.

Lenton, R., Smith, M.D., Fox, J. and Morra, N. (1999) 'Sexual harassment in public places: experiences of Canadian women', *Canadian Review of Sociology*, 36, pp 517–40.

Lewis, R., Sharp, E., Remnant, J. and Redpath, R. (2015) '"Safe spaces": experiences of feminist women-only space', *Sociological Research Online*, 20(4), pp 1–14.

Liska, A.E., Sanchirico, A., and Reed, M.D. (1988) 'Fear of crime and constrained behavior specifying and estimating a reciprocal effects model', *Social Forces*, 66(3), pp 827–37.

2
27

Lorde, A. (2007) *Sister Outsider: Essays and Speeches by Audre Lorde*, Berkeley, CA: Crossing Press.

Lundgren, E. (1998) 'The Hand that Strikes and Comforts: Gender Construction and the Tension Between Body and Soul', in Dobash, R.E, and Dobash, R.P. (eds) *Rethinking Violence Against Women*, Thousand Oaks, CA: Sage, pp 169–98.

Madriz, E. (1997a) *Nothing Bad Happens to Good Girls: Fear of Crime in Women's Lives*, Berkeley, CA: University of California Press.

Madriz, E. (1997b) 'Images of criminals and victims: A study on women's fear and social control', *Gender and Society*, 11(3), pp 342–56.

McGlynn, C. and Rackley, E. (2017) 'Image-based sexual abuse', *Oxford Journal of Legal Studies*, 37(3), pp 534–61.

McNeil, S. (1987) 'Flashing: Its effect on women', in Hanmer, J. and Maynard, M. (eds) *Women, Violence and Social Control*, Basingstoke: Macmillan, pp 93–109.

Merleau-Ponty, M. (2002) *Phenomenology of Perception*, translated by C. Smith, Oxford: Routledge.

Miriam, K. (2007) 'Toward a Phenomenology of Sex-Right: Reviving Radical Feminist Theory of Compulsory Heterosexuality', *Hypatia*, 22(1), pp 210–28.

Msonza, N. (2014) 'Reflections on the Zimbabwe Mini Skirt March', *Her Zimbabwe*, 23 December, www.herzimbabwe.co.zw/2014/12/reflections-on-the-zimbabwe-miniskirt-march.

Oakley, A. (1974) *The Sociology of Housework*, New York: Pantheon Books.

Office for National Statistics (2016) Compendium: Focus on Violent Crime and Sexual Offending Year ending March 2015, www.ons.gov.uk/peoplepopulationandcommunity/crimeandjustice/compendium/focusonviolentcrimeandsexualoffences/yearendingmarch2015/chapter4intimatepersonalviolenceandpartnerabuse

Pain, R. (2001) 'Gender, race, age and fear in the city', *Urban Studies*, 38(5–6), pp 899–913.

Phadke, S., Khan, S. and Ranade, S. (2011) *Why Loiter?: Women and Risk on Mumbai Streets*, New Delhi: Penguin Books India.

Plath, S. (2000) *The Unabridged Journals of Sylvia Plath*, edited by Karen V. Kukil, New York: Anchor.

Regan, L. and Kelly, L. (2003) *'Rape: Still a forgotten issue'. Briefing Document for Strengthening the Linkages: Consolidating the European Network Project*. Child and Woman Abuse Studies Unit, London Metropolitan University.

Rich, A. (1979) *On Lies, Secrets, and Silence*, New York: Norton.

Riger, S. and Gordon, M.T. (1981) 'The fear of rape: A study in social control', *Journal of Social Issues*, 37(4), pp. 71–92.

Rogers, C. (1961) *On Becoming a Person: A Therapist's View of Psychotherapy*, London: Constable.

Rollins, J. (1985) *Between Women: Domestics and Their Employers*, Philadelphia: Temple University Press.

Salter, M. (2013) 'Justice and revenge in online counter-publics: Emerging responses to sexual violence in the age of social media', *Crime, Media, Culture*, 9(3), pp 225–42.

Sanghani, R. (2015) 'Police rape prevention poster 'blames sexual assault victims'', *Telegraph*, 8 April, www.telegraph.co.uk/women/womens-life/11522485/Police-rape-prevention-poster-blames-sexual-assault-victims.html

Schepple, K., and Bart, P. (1983) 'Through Women's Eyes: Defining Danger in the Wake of Sexual Assault', *Journal of Social Issues*, 39 (2), pp 63–80.

Seith, C., and Kelly, L. (2003) *Achievements Against the Grain: Self-Defence Training for Women and Girls in Europe*, Child and Woman Abuse Studies Unit, London Metropolitan University.

Senn, C.Y., Eliasziw, M., Barata, P.C., Thurston, W.E., Newby-Clark, I.R., Radtke, H.L. and Hobden, K.L. (2015) 'Efficacy of a sexual assault resistance program for university women', *The New England Journal of Medicine*, 372, pp 2326–35.

Shoukry, A., Hassan, R. and Komsan, N.A. (2008) *Clouds in Egypt's Sky, Sexual Harassment: From Verbal Harassment to Rape*, Cairo: Egyptian Center for Women's Rights (ECWR), www.endvawnow.org/uploads/browser/files/ecrw_sexual_harassment_study_english.pdf.pdf.

Smith, M.D. (1988) 'Women's fear of violent crime: An exploratory test of a feminist hypothesis', *Journal of Family Violence*, 3(1), pp 29–38.

Somers, J. (2015) 'Essex Police Defend Student Safety Poster Campaign After Petition Brands It 'Victim Blaming'', Huffington Post UK, 29 September, www.huffingtonpost.co.uk/2015/09/29/essex-police-deny-claims_n_8214272.html

Spender, D. (1985) *Man Made Language* (2nd edition), New York: Routledge and Kegan Paul.

Stanko. E. (1990) *Everyday Violence: Women's and Men's Experience of Personal Danger*, London: Pandora Press.

Stanko, E.A. (1993a) 'Ordinary Fear: Women, Violence, and Personal Safety', in P.B. Bart and E.G. Moran (eds) *Violence Against Women: The Bloody Footprints*, Newbury Park: Sage, pp 155–64.

Stanko, E.A. (1993b) 'The case of fearful women: Gender, personal safety and fear of crime', *Women and Criminal Justice*, 4(1), pp 117–35.

Stanko, E.A. (1995) 'Women, crime, and fear', *The Annals of the American Academy of Political and Social Science*, 539(1), pp 46–58.

Stark, E. (2009) 'Rethinking Coercive Control', *Violence Against Women,* 15 (12), pp 1509–25.

Sutton, R.M. and Farrall, S. (2004) 'Gender, socially desirable responding and the fear of crime: Are women really more anxious about crime?', *British Journal of Criminology*, 45(2), pp 212–24.

Time (2017) '700,000 Female Farmworkers Say They Stand With Hollywood Actors Against Sexual Assault', 10 November, http://time.com/5018813/farmworkers-solidarity-hollywood-sexual-assault

Vera-Gray, F. (2016a) 'Men's stranger intrusions: rethinking street harassment', *Women's Studies International Forum*, 58, pp 9–17.

Vera-Gray, F. (2016b) 'Situating Agency', Trouble and Strife, www.troubleandstrife.org/2016/05/situating-agency/

Vera-Gray, F. (2017a) *Men's Intrusion, Women's Embodiment: A Critical Analysis of Street Harassment*, Oxford: Routledge.

Vera-Gray, F. (2017b) 'Girlhood, agency, and embodied space for action', in Formark, B., Mulari, H. and Voipio, M. (eds) *Nordic Girlhoods: New Perspectives and Outlooks*, New York: Palgrave Macmillan, pp 127–35.

Warr, M. (1985) 'Fear of rape among urban women', *Social Problems*, 32(3), pp 238–50.

WCLRF (2015) *Research on Sexual Harassment Against Women in Public Places, Workplace and Educational Institutions of Afghanistan*, Kabul: Women and Children Legal Research Foundation.

Wignall, L. (2015) 'Can anti-rape poster campaigns help prevent attacks?', BBC Newsbeat, 8 April, www.bbc.co.uk/newsbeat/article/32219357/can-anti-rape-poster-campaigns-help-prevent-attacks

Wise, S. and Stanley, L. (1987) *Georgie Porgie: Sexual Harassment in Everyday Life*, London: Pandora Press.

World Health Organization, Department of Reproductive Health and Research, London School of Hygiene and Tropical Medicine (2013) *Global and regional estimates of violence against women: Prevalence and health effects of intimate partner violence and non-partner violence*. Italy: World Health Organization.

Index

Note: [P] following index entry denotes research participant.